COUNSELING PARENTS OF EXCEPTIONAL CHILDREN:

Principles, Problems
and Procedures

Jack C. Stewart, Ed.D.
Columbus College
Columbus, Georgia

MSS EDUCATIONAL PUBLISHING COMPANY, INC.
655 Madison Ave., New York, N. Y. 10021

Library of Congress Cataloging in Publication Data

Stewart, Jack C
    Counseling parents of exceptional children.

    1. Exceptional children. 2. Parent and child.
3. Counseling. 4. Children — Management — Study and
teaching. I. Title. [DNLM: 1. Counseling.
2. Handicapped. 3. Parent — Child relations. WS107
S849c]
HQ773.S67   371.9   74-10596
ISBN 0-8422-0422-9 (pbk.)

CONTENTS

FOREWORD

Programs in the field of special education have been making dramatic progress over the past few years. Beginning with the massive involvement of the Federal government in the 1960's, a new focus has been generated for programs for handicapped children and youth. Recent court cases regarding the equal right to an education for all children increase the need for a constant up-dating of our approaches to all children.

This text will be a valuable addition to the progress that is rapidly being made in the education of exceptional children. Great attention is being placed on the importance of the preschool years for all children, and the need for training for the exceptional child takes on an even greater impetus when one views recent research endeavors. The wave of interest in the education of children in the early years will cause some concern for educators who have been programmed to accept these children on certain levels of readiness when entering public schools. Changing legislation being enacted throughout the country shall shift the emphasis downward. Practical, meaningful methods are a necessity to assist those educators and professionals already employed. Simultaneously, pre-service preparation must be held accountable so that future educators possess resources and information regarding parent counseling that until recent years were not emphasized.

By stressing the fundamentals of counseling as well as the practical application of principles and procedures, this text will make a contribution in the areas of teacher preparation and both pre-service and in-service training as related to effective working relationships between the professional and parents of exceptional children. Constant improvement of professional personnel and others concerned with the exceptional child is a paramount concern and this text will make a major contribution in that direction.

Wilson L. Dietrich
Professor and Chairman
Department of Special Education
and Rehabilitation
College of Education
Memphis State University

PREFACE

This book is written for three specific purposes. First, it will serve as an up-dated, relatively inexpensive resource guide for the varied professional personnel whose daily work rests upon establishing and maintaining effective relationships with parents of exceptional children. This includes but is not limited to such personnel as special education teachers, regular teachers, mental health workers, guidance counselors and psychologists. The contents of this text can also be used for preservice and inservice training sessions to upgrade expertise in counseling and thereby provide a more effective delivery of counseling services to parents of exceptional children. In order to more effectively fulfill the purposes of both an inservice activity and a college text, problems for class discussion and individual inquiry are suggested at the conclusion of each chapter. This should add an extra dimension for those who wish to go beyond the written word and "think" about the specifics related to each chapter.

Secondly, this book should serve as a suitable text for the undergraduate or graduate student who is entering one of the many fields in special education or a program in counselor education. As the number of teacher training programs in special education continues to expand, there seems to be ample evidence there will be an increased emphasis on the why and how of counseling parents of exceptional children.

Lastly, after having twice attempted to teach a course entitled "Counseling Parents of Exceptional Children," it became rather evident that (in my opinion) a text was not available which combined the two factors so essential for expertise in this area. The two factors are: (1) an understanding of the theoretical and practical aspects of the counseling process, and (2) a general exploration of the multitude of personal, social, educational and economic problems and challenges that will be faced in one way or another by all parents of exceptional children. All of the textbooks previewed by this writer gave a heavy emphasis to only one of the factors mentioned above, usually emphasizing parental attitudes toward mental retardation and/or another handicapping condition.

This volume is not intended to be comprehensive; it by no means tries to cover every facet related to the effective counseling of parents of exceptional children. Rather it attempts to explore a limited number of basic themes, with the object of forming a clear conceptual framework for understanding the role and function of the person who seeks to effectively counsel parents of exceptional children.

This book is committed to the idea that professional workers in the various disciplines have both the potential and the capability to foster and promote genuine understanding, acceptance, and realistic expectations through effective counseling of parents of exceptional children. Some recent research suggests that even minimally trained or even lay counselors can obtain results no different from those of fully-trained professional counselors. The reader should not expect to find magic formulas or prescriptions that will cover all cases. Because we are speaking of relationships with human beings, no situation will ever be exactly the same as another. When we think we have experienced everything, we invariably meet something new. However, the professional's thoughtful, skillful, utilization of counseling can, and will, enhance the parent's grasp of the situation by strengthening interpersonal relationships and thereby contributing substantially to the proposition that effective counseling is concerned with the total development of each individual. It is toward this end that this book is presented.

I wish to thank all of the people who have been helpful in the preparation of this book. With never a word of complaint Miss Marcia Case cheerfully and skillfully typed out the several versions of the manuscript. Special appreciation is extended to Mrs. Rinda Brewbaker for her thoughtful criticism and careful editing. I would also like to thank Dr. Frances Duncan for the generous loan of books and materials from her professional library. Finally, the author is indebted to Dr. Charles Parker, Chairman of the Education Division, Columbus College, for his encouragement and support in this type of endeavor.

INTRODUCTION

With the increased and continued emphasis on providing services for exceptional children, perhaps at no time in the history of this country has there been a greater need for the effective counseling and education of parents of exceptional children. In his Education of the Exceptional Child, B.R. Gearheart [1] discusses trends in Special Education and predicts a major increase in emphasis on educational intervention through work with parents. According to Gearheart, parent education will take many directions, but two emphasis appear certain. The first is a more accurate conceptualization of the ramifications of the child's disabilty and various likely resultant handicaps. For example, the parent of a deaf child does not understand all of the educational and social handicaps which will soon face his child unless he is helped to do so.

The second emphasis involves developing the parent into an efficient "teacher aide." The point here, according to Gearheart, is that the child spends a larger percentage of his waking hours at home than in a school program. In this respect, Dr. Benjamin Bloom [2], the eminent psychologist at the University of Chicago, has made an analysis of hundreds of studies dealing with intelligence, achievement, physical traits, interests, attitudes and personality. With respect to general intelligence measured at age 17, Bloom concluded that a child develops 80 percent of his mature intelligence between conception and age eight, half by the time he is four years old and the remaining 20 percent from ages eight to seventeen. Studies such as these clearly indicate that the home environment is the single most critical influence on a child's development during the preschool years. Given guidance and direction, parents can become effective teacher aides and thereby assist in their child's intellectual, social and emotional growth.

It seems evident that programs involving intervention into the home are developing rapidly and will become more extensive in practice throughout the 1970's. If professionals take adequate readings from current research, we cannot afford to do less than prepare ourselves for the challenging task that lies before us.

PROBLEMS FOR INDIVIDUAL STUDY AND CLASS DISCUSSION

1. Do you support or refute Gearheart's contention that we will see a major increase in parent intervention? What evidence can you cite to support your viewpoint?

2. What factors (political, economic, social, educational, etc.) can you see as having a direct influence on the scope and involvement of parent intervention?

3. Debate: Because of the special problems that a handicapped condition brings, intervention for the parent of the exceptional child is more important and should receive a higher priority than home intervention for parents of the "normal" child.

4. If financial resources and trained personnel were unlimited, design a master plan for your local school/community in which parents of exceptional children would be involved in individual or group counseling programs on a regular basis. What problems related to human relationships would you expect to encounter? Why? Would you expect to encounter administrative problems? What might be the nature of these problems?

5. Would you include parents of the culturally disadvantaged in your master plan? Why or why not?

REFERENCES

1. Gearheart, B.R. Education of the Exceptional Child. Scranton, Penn.: International Textbook, 1972, pp. 363-364.

2. Bloom, B.S. Stability and Change in Human Characteristics. New York: John Wiley and Sons, 1964, p. 137.

PART ONE

PROFESSIONAL COUNSELING

Introduction to Part I

Counseling may be viewed as a process by which one person
(the counselor) helps another person (the counselee or client)
to deal more effectively not only with his inner world of
feelings but also with the stresses imposed by the impact of
other people and his physical environment. Maximum effectiveness will be achieved when the counselor views his task as facilitating and supporting, rather than as teaching and persuading. Part I of this text is intended to identify, and discuss, and elaborate upon the skills and techniques that constitute effective counseling. This section is also committed
to the idea that professionals can and do enter into counseling with parents of exceptional children and that parents can
find in counselors some of the support and courage needed as
they embark upon the counseling relationship. Effective counseling is not predicated upon "guesswork" or "hunches", but is
and should be based upon the best scientific knowledge at our
disposal. Only after evidence of a constructive behavior
change in the client can we lay rightful claim to being effective professional counselors.

Chapter 1

OVERVIEW OF COUNSELING

The Nature of Effective Counseling

This section begins with a very fundamental question: What is counseling? Since a major portion of this book is about the counseling process and those who practice it, some definitions of counseling seem to be in order especially if its working boundries are to be established. A problem which arises immediately is the fact that from a historical perspective counseling has become equated with the giving of advice. To confuse matters even more, this idea is still prevalent and is the cause of much conflict and confusion when the counselors in educational and non-educational settings do not view their function as parceling out advice. The situation is not helped when those in search of help are offered aid by many types of persons who call themselves "counselors." For example, there are investment counselors, financial counselors, burial counselors, automotive counselors and used-car counselors.

It can be seen that counseling has gradually evolved into a catch-all term used to denote a variety of practices including encouragement, the giving of advice and information, testing and test interpretation, and even the highly technical field of psychoanalysis. In order to establish a more accurate conceptualization of counseling, a representative sampling of definitions of counseling in the literature begins here. They reflect many of the subtle differences that have evolved in recent years. Obviously, counseling does not lend itself to easy definition.

. . . A definitely structured permissive relationship which allows the client to gain an understanding of himself to a degree which enables him to take positive steps in the light of his new orientation [1]

. . . A relationship in which one person endeavors to help another to understand and solve his adjustment problem [2]

. . . . A process which takes place in a one-to-one relationship between an individual troubled by problems
with which he cannot cope alone, and a professional
worker whose training and experience have qualified
him to help others reach solutions to various types
of personal experiences [3]

. . . . That interaction which (a) occurs between two individuals called a counselor and client, (b) takes
place in a professional setting, and (c) is ini-
tiated and maintained as a means of facilitating
changes in the behavior of a client [4]

. . . . Helping an individual become aware of himself and
the ways in which he reacts to the behavioral influences of his environment. It further helps him
to establish some personal meaning for this behavior and to develop and clarify a set of goals and
values for further behavior [5]

. . . . A process by which a troubled person (the client) is
helped to feel and behave in a more personally satis-
fying manner through interaction with an uninvolved
person (the counselor) who provides information and
reactions which stimulate the client to develop behaviors which enable him to deal more effectively
with himself and his environment [6]

By contrast, it is interesting to note what Patterson [7] says
counseling is "not":

1. Counseling does not merely consist of the giving of information, though information may be a part of the process.

2. By the same token, counseling is not the giving of
advice and pointing out what the client should do in
any given situation.

3. Counseling is not the influencing of attitudes, beliefs
or behavior by means of persuading, leading, or con-
vincing.

4. Counseling is not the influencing of behavior by admonishing, warning, threatening, or compelling without the use of physical force or coercion.

5. Counseling is not interviewing (while interviewing is involved, it is not synonymous).

What then is the nature of counseling? What are its goals and purposes? Let us examine these questions in more detail. Advocating a developmental approach, Mathewson [8] contents that the counselor has the responsibility to "help his counselee to become a valuing person in his own right, and to understand the values he wants to live by, and to choose and act accordingly."

Proposing that counseling centers on helping individuals live as "whole persons," Carkhuff and Berenson [9] say that "the life of a whole person is made up of actions fully integrating his emotional, intellectual and physical resources in such a way that these actions lead to greater and greater self-definition." They list the following as general statements reflecting the implications of becoming whole:

1. The only consistency for the whole person is internal.

2. Creativity and honesty are a way of life for the whole person.

3. Although the way the whole person lives his life is seen by others to be dangerous, too intense, and too profound, he is in tune with the fact that his real risk involves living life without risk.

4. The whole person realizes that life is empty without acting.

5. The whole person realizes that whatever he does is worth doing well.

6. The whole and creative person functions at a high energy level.

7. The whole person comes to the realization that few men are large enough or whole enough to love and nourish the creative person.

8. The whole person is fully aware that any significant human relationship is in the process of deepening or deteriorating.

9. The whole person realizes that most men say "yes" out of fear of the implications of saying "no," and that most men say "no" out of fear of the implications of saying "yes."

10. The whole person is fully aware that in order to live life in such a way that it is a continuous learning and relearning process, he must periodically burn bridges behind him.

11. The whole person realizes that he is, and must be, his own pathfinder, and travel a road never traveled before.

12. The whole person does not fear living intensely.

13. The whole person is prepared to face the implications of functioning a step ahead or above most of those with whom he comes into contact.

14. The whole person is aware that for most people life is a cheap game.

15. The whole person is fully aware that many of society's rewards are designed to render the creative impotent.

16. The whole person realizes that to emerge within the acceptable levels tolerated by society means institutionalization.

17. The whole person realizes that he must escape traps to render him impotent.

18. The whole person is aware of the awesome responsibility which comes with freedom.

In 1960 Curran [10] spoke of the counseling process as a search for values. From this frame of reference, the client's self-search leads to ultimate questions related to the meaning of life. The counselor's goal, according to Curran, should be to assist the client in his search and allow him to make his own goal choices.

16

For the individual, this means trying to find the answers
to three key questions: Who am I? Where am I Going? Why?
According to Coleman [11] these questions deal with one's self-
concept, one's life plans, and one's value patterns - in essence
with the self-knowledge, goals and competencies, and value judg-
ments involved in self-direction.

Peterson [12] raises a significant question: Are there any
commonly agreed-upon values among counselors? To answer this
question two assumptions must be made: Since any school of counseling or psychotherapy grows out of a particular culture in response to specific needs, it would seem logical that the basic
values of that culture would be strongly reflected in its ethical
position. In our society it is not surprising then to discover
general agreement among counselors upon key values involving the
individual and his worth. The second critical point is recognition of the fact that the way counselors deal with the problems
they are confronted with varies according to the particular counseling approach they have developed for themselves. While this
idea will be explored in detail later, suffice it to say that different people counsel differently.

The Goals of Counseling

At the risk of omitting several important considerations,
there seems to be general agreement as to the goals and purposes
of counseling at the abstract level. Some of these are summarized
below:

> Counseling is a learning process and involves the
> establishment of a relationship in which one person
> (the counselor) helps another (the client) to deal more
> effectively with himself and the situational demands of
> his environment. It should be noted that group counsel-
> ing has come of age and will be treated in a later sec-
> tion. At the conclusion of the counseling session, the
> client is different from what he was before the relation-
> ship.

> The counselor maintains a firm and abiding faith in
> the worth and dignity of the individual and believes that
> people can change their behavior - why else would they
> counsel?

The counselor upholds the right to choose his own values in the process of self-discovery. As one examines several counseling approaches, the trend seems to be toward assigning more responsibility to the counselee.

The counseling process may be carried on by persons who are not necessarily professional counselors. While this is a risky proposition, the entire thrust of this book holds that effective counseling can take place as the result of a unique relationship established between the counselor and the client. Formal or professional training is desirable but by no means essential.

Counseling is normally conducted by a disinterested person in private and all discussion/information should be considered confidential.

Within the context of this book, counseling is an activity that addresses itself primarily to normal problems of human development. In this light, counseling may be spoken of as "developmental facilitation," a means whereby the counselor assists the counselee in increasing his coping skills and thereby decreasing difficulties which come about in the developmental processes.

Counseling is one of the helping professions. McCully [13] noting the absence of an authoritative definition had this to say:

A helping relationship is defined as one which, based upon its specialized knowledge, applies an intellectual technique to the existential affairs of others toward the end of enabling them to cope more effectively with the dilemma and paradoxes that characterize the human condition.

Carl Rogers [14] has described the helping relationship with great clarity through a series of probing questions:

Can I be in some way which will be perceived by the other person as trustworthy, as dependable or consistent in some deep sense?

Can I be expressive enough as a person that what I am will be communicated unambiguously?

Can I let myself experience positive attitudes toward this other person - attitudes of warmth, caring, liking, interest, respect?

18

Can I be strong enough as a person to be separate from the other?

Am I secure enough within myself to permit him his separateness?

Can I let myself enter fully into the world of his feelings and personal meaning and see those as he does?

Can I receive him as he is? Can I communicate this attitude?

Can I act with sufficient sensitivity in the relationship that my behavior will not be perceived as a threat?

Can I free him from the threat of external evaluation?

Can I meet this other person who is in the process of becoming, or will I be bound by his past and by my past?

Finally, counseling is essentially human interaction and a unique human relationship. According to Munson [15], the counselor can provide an opportunity for others to examine their feelings, attitudes, values, and beliefs and the manner in which they express these in day-to-day behavior. He can provide conditions of acceptance, understanding, and trust. The counselor doesn't do these things just in a counseling cubicle; he tries to be a person and to relate to others in "human" ways.

Admittedly, counseling is difficult to define concisely to the liking of everyone. Hopefully, this chapter has provided an overview and thereby a rationale and basis for the development of "your" personal views as to what counseling is and what its goals are.

PROBLEMS FOR INDIVIDUAL STUDY AND CLASS DISCUSSION

1. How important is it that the working boundaries of counseling be established?

2. Of the definitions of counseling presented in this chapter, which one do you find personally most appealing? Why? Least appealing? Why?

3. Devise your own concept or definition of counseling. Defend it in terms of purpose, comprehensiveness, clarity, and your concept of what counseling should or should not be.

4. Debate: Resolved - A counselor (by definition) serves a unique function and therefore should have formal (professional) training prior to counseling with parents of exceptional children.

5. Look back at the questions that Rogers proposed as facilitating the helping relationship. On a continuum from 0 to 10, rate yourself as to how your feelings measure up to these questions. As this is a self-evaluation exercise, honesty is essential.

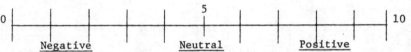

For example, if because of your intense interest in other people and your desire to help, you do not feel you are strong enough a person to be separate from the other, you may give yourself a 2 on this on this characteristic.

Now go back and carefully analyze your responses. If your responses were for the most part in the positive zone (6 through 10), you may be Roger's ideal person who works effectively in the helping relationship.

If some of or most of your responses were in the negative zone (0 through 4), carefully analyze each question in light of possible explanations. You might consider such factors as experience, training, the complexity of the helping relationship, or factors relating to your own personality (attitudes, beliefs, values and lack of openness and acceptance). It is important to remember that, in the final analysis, the counselor is left to himself to decide how he will deal with the counseling relationship. In this regard, it would be tragic for the counselor to remain ignorant of his own values and personality make-up.

6. Discuss what is meant by maintaining a firm and abiding faith in the worth and dignity of the individual. As an outside activity, collect ideas from such individuals such as Earl C. Kelley, Carl R. Rogers, Abraham H. Maslow, and Arthur W. Combs. How do they define the helping relationship? How does respect for the individual enhance the relationship?

7. Counseling is a way of understanding problems better, not
    solving them. What reasons can you think of to support
    or refute this statement?

REFERENCES

1. Rogers, C.R. Counseling and Psychotherapy. Boston:
    Houghton Mifflin, 1942, p. 18.

2. English, H.B. and A.C. A Comprehensive Dictionary of
    Psychological and Psychoanalytical Terms. New York:
    David McKay, 1958, p. 127.

3. Smith, G.E. Counseling in the Secondary School. New York:
    Macmillan, 1955, p. 156.

4. Pepinsky, H. and Pepinsky, P. Counseling Theory and Practice.
    New York: Roland Press, 1954, p. 3.

5. Blocker, D.H. Developmental Counseling. New York: Roland
    Press, 1966, p. 5.

6. Lewis, E.C. The Psychology of Counseling. New York:
    Holt, Rinehart, and Winston, 1970, p. 10.

7. Patterson, C.H., ed. The Counselor in the School. New York:
    McGraw-Hill, 1967, pp. 219-227.

8. Mathewson, R.H. Guidance Policy and Practice. 3rd Edition.
    New York: Harper and Row, 1962, p. 161.

9. Carkhuff, R.R. and Berenson, B.G. Beyond Counseling and
    Therapy. New York: Holt, Rinehart, and Winston,
    1967, p. 197.

10. Curran, C.A. "Some Ethical and Scientific Values in the
    Counseling Psychotherapeutic Process," Personnel and
    Guidance Journal, XXXIX, 1 (September, 1960), 15-20.

11. Coleman, J.A. Psychology and Effective Behavior. Glenview,
    Illinois: Scott Foresman and Co., p. 7.

12. Peterson, J.A. Counseling and Values. Scranton: Pennsylvania:
    International Textbook, 1970, p. 117.

13. McCully, C.H. "Conceptions of Man and the Helping Professions," Personnel and Guidance Journal, Vol. 44 (May, 1966). p. 912.

14. Rogers, C.R. On Becoming a Person. Boston: Houghton Mifflin, Co., 1961, pp. 50-55.

15. Munson, H.L. Foundations of Developmental Guidance. Boston: Allyn and Bacon, 1971, p. 116.

Chapter 2

COUNSELOR ATTITUDES AND CHARACTERISTICS

This chapter will focus on some of the significant traits and characteristics which are usually associated with the effective counselor. The direction and outcome of any counseling session may be heavily influenced by counselor attitudes. The attitudes of the counselor and his approaches toward the individual as well as what he does all have a tremendous bearing on the success or failure of the counseling relationship. The main thesis of this text is that a mature individual can be a successful counselor capable of bringing about constructive behavior change in the client. It is, therefore, imperative that attention be given to some of the traits usually attributed to skilled counselors.

Research tells us that there is no single ideal counselor Personality. As a matter of fact, many kinds of people can and do become effective counselors. One must also keep in mind that as a prospective or even a practicing counselor, one must not expect to be equally effective with all clients.

Despite the fact that the counselor cannot be all things to all people, it is important to consider briefly some of the major traits which are suggested as desirable counselor traits. Keep in mind that a counselor may have a deficiency in one or more areas and still be able to become an effective counselor. The discussion of traits which follows would only indicate that the greater a person's proficiency in these areas, the greater the likelihood that he will be successful in establishing a meaningful relationship and bringing about behavior change in the client. The intent, then, is not to come up with a list of absolutes which the counselor must either fulfill or aspire to achieve, but to stimulate thinking at a very personal level and seek to respond to the question - what kind of person should the counselor be and what are some of the traits and characteristics he should possess? Hopefully, as a result of inner probing, the reader will be provoked into a serious self-examination that will enable him to (more clearly) recognize his own personality traits and attempt to determine how his own personality traits may be related to the effectiveness of any counseling relationship.

Interest in Helping People

One basic characteristic of the successful counselor is that he likes people. If he doesn't, his success as a "helping person" is very limited. The prospective counselor must have the courage to honestly and openly ask himself if he likes people and not be afraid of what he may discover about his true convictions in this regard. Counseling is one of the helping professions and the counselor simply must be or seek to be one who helps in spirit and action as well as word. As Coleman [1] so aptly describes it, caring deeply for something outside oneself is one of the most gratifying and self-fulfilling of human experiences. The counselor who does not like people multiplies his work and minimizes his effectiveness.

Adequate Personal Adjustment

While there is no agreement as to the extent that counselors should themselves be free of personal problems, Lewis [2] offers the suggestion that the counselor should be able to deal with his problems in a constructive manner and not attempt to help clients deal with problems with which he himself is having trouble. Of prime importance here is the individual's self-concept, for whether it is accurate or not, he assumes it is and acts accordingly.

Acceptance

First and foremost, acceptance requires respect for the client as a person of worth. This is best illustrated by Rogers' [3] definition of acceptance:

> By acceptance I mean a warm regard for him as a person of unconditional self-worth - of value no matter what his condition, his behavior or his feelings. It means a respect and liking for him as a separate person, a willingness for him to possess his own feelings in his own way. It means an acceptance of a regard for his attitudes of the moment, no matter how negative or positive, no matter how much they may contradict other attitudes he has held in the past.

Acceptance should be demonstrated by the counselor and client; each must be willing to accept the basic nature and characteristics of the other. Furthermore, each should behave in ways that convey the thought "I accept you."

In much the same vein, as a prerequisite to accepting the counselee, the counselor must understand and accept himself. Sometimes a role conflict occurs in which what he sees himself to be as a person may run contrary to how he functions as a counselor. As Yates and Smith [4] remark:

It sometimes happens that the counselor intellectually recognizes a need to be accepting and understanding and in his self-concept must be such a person. If in the perception of the client he is not, the relationship will become confusing to both the client and the counselor. But if the counselor is willing and able to accept what the client says as it pertains to the counseling relationship, he may begin to see himself as the client sees him.

Trust is closely akin to acceptance but more abstract. Trust is manifested by confidence in another person. Munson [5] points out the importance of trust in the counseling relationship:

A counselor must be trusting - this is, he must trust others. If he is unable to trust others in his own living, it is difficult to transfer this lack of trust outside the counseling relationship to one of trust in it. This feeling of trust, then, is something that the counselor must experience himself in order that the other person can feel free and able to reciprocate and respond in the process of communication.

Understanding/Empathy

It is a truism that everyone desires to be understood. The counselor must, therefore, understand the counselee if the relationship is to be beneficial. As Benjamin [6] described it, this calls for putting aside everything but our common humanness and with it alone trying to understand with the other person how he thinks, feels, and sees the world around him.

It is especially important that the beginning counselor realize that the question is not to agree or disagree, but to understand with the other person how he thinks, feels, and sees the world around him. It means ridding ourselves of our internal frame of reference and adopting his.

Many writers refer to this process as "empathy", which is frequently described as putting oneself in the other person's shoes. The recognition and awareness of attitudes, thoughts, feeling, and perceptions between counselor and client are an integral part of an empathic understanding. Obviously, understanding and empathy are closely akin in meaning. In both situations, the counselor "feels with" the counselee. In most cases, this is what the client needs. The rule is, when we feel empathy toward another person, we are conveying a simple yet meaningful message to that person. We are in effect saying, "I understand," not "I feel sorry for you." Feeling sorry implies that we may feel superior and more fortunate in some way. The parent of a handicapped child needs our understanding, our empathy. He doesn't need or want us to feel sorry for him. As one counsels with parents, he must have (or develop) an ability to, so far as humanly possible, understand the client's meanings and feelings. For example, the parent may strenuously object to what the counselor feels is a logical course of action. If the counselor perceives this as stubborn, foolish, or primitive behavior, the counselor has failed to develop a sensitivity of the client's attitudes and he will likely be unable to assist the client in any genuine, meaningful ways. In most cases, professional and parents are working toward the same goal-the maximum development and adjustment of the child. What is needed is mutual respect, understanding, and empathy.

Rapport

According to Shertzer and Stone, [7] rapport is described simply as a condition essential to a comfortable and unconditional relationship between counselor and counselee. It is established and maintained through the counselor's genuine interest in and acceptance of the client. It cannot be forced or contrived. It is a bond characterized by interest, responsiveness, and sensitive humanistic involvement.

The establishment of rapport is vital to the success of any counseling relationship. It is of particular importance during the initial counseling session when both counselor and client may be uncertain about the role expectations of the other. As an operational concept, rapport sounds rather easy to accomplish, but rapport goes beyond a friendly greeting and the attempt to make the counselee feel comfortable and at ease. In this respect, Shertzer and Stone make the following comment:

"Unfortunately, rapport is an intangible entity characterized by pleasantness, confidence, cooperation, sincerity and interest - all qualities difficult to initiate by recipe or by a
bag of tricks."

Genuineness/Honesty

In order to promote a genuine relationship, the counselor
should be, in the words of Carl Rogers, a "real person" to his
client. He should always strive to be himself - an authentic
person interested in helping the other person. Honesty and
genuineness cannot be turned on and off like a faucet, but must
be a unique part of one's total personality. Closely related to genuineness is the counselor's personal security and
stability. If the counselor feels secure, he is more likely to
be himself in the counseling relationship.

Attentiveness/Listening

A fundamental rule for the effective counselor is attentiveness. In this context, attentiveness demands full involvement of the client's verbal and non-verbal communications. Attentiveness beyond the superficial level requires the use of
one invaluable tool: listening. Lest the reader view listening
skills lightly, genuine listening is hard work and there is
little about it that is mechanical. Furthermore, it is the
author's viewpoint that people in general do not know how to
listen effectively. It should also be noted that listening is
closely tied to acceptance and understanding in that listening
conveys to the client that the counselor is interested in and
sensitive to his concerns. As a historical note, the recognition for the need to listen goes back some 4,400 years ago when
Prahhotep, one of the pharoahs, instructed the viziers and of-
ficers of his staff as follows: "An official who must listen to
the pleas of clients should listen patiently and without rancor,
because a petitioner wants attention to what he says even more
than the accomplishing of that for which he came" [8]. In a
real sense, the counselor's most important tool is listening.
This becomes even more vital when the nondirective approach to
counseling is used. More about this will follow in Chapter 4.

It should be acknowledged that listening is often not
enough. The physical interaction between counselor and client
can also be meaningful. Both counselor and counselee may learn

much about the other through non-verbal communication, i.e., facial expressions, posture, eye-contact, gestures, and body movements.

Know Human Behavior

This discussion of desirable counselor characteristics will conclude with the contention that the counselor should be knowledgeable in the fundamental facets of human behavior. As one writer has said: "Our task as counselors is to represent our understanding of the human dynamics of learning and to work to see that these insights are incorporated into the learning environment" [9]. In a provocative article by Berdie,[10] a viewpoint is expressed that counseling as we now know it will be replaced by another discipline called applied behavioral science. The applied behavioral scientist would be well versed in social influence theory, reinforcement theory, cognitive development theories, field theory, psychoanalytic theory, trait-and factor theory, role theory, and decision theory. Obviously, we now know more about human behavior than ever before. Effective counselors can and should use this knowledge to help people avoid costly and needless mistakes and the wasting of their potential for self-fulfillment. The question is - are we willing to expend the time and effort needed to increase our understanding about the dynamics of human behavior? The successful counselor cannot afford to do anything less.

PROBLEMS FOR INDIVIDUAL STUDY AND CLASS DISCUSSION

1. Can you think of other counselor characteristics which are desirable and need to be discussed.

2. Describe, in your own words, the "ideal" counselor.

3. Think of a person who once assisted you in a helping relationship. What characteristics did this person possess which enabled him to bring about a change in your behavior?

4. Rank from most important to least important, the counselor characteristics discussed in this chapter. Beside each characteristic, write a brief statement or comment to defend and support your selections.

5. What reasons can you think of to support the contention that learning to understand is not an easy process?

6. In the spaces below, list some verbal responses that would convey empathic understanding to a client.

a. _____

b. _____

c. _____

d. _____

e. _____

DISCUSS YOUR RESPONSES WITH SOMEONE.

7. Skill in careful listening is not acquired by accident. Can you think of some practical suggestions as to how listening skills can be improved?

8. There is considerable evidence that self-acceptance and the acceptance of others are related and that individuals who are self-accepting are usually more accepting of others. What are the implications of this statement? How can one increase his self-acceptance? List some characteristics of self-accepting individuals.

9. How does one handle emotional scenes? They are bound to come at one point or another in your work with parents of exceptional children.

10. Can rapport be taught or does it come about from being able to empathize with others?

11. Do some personality characteristics influence counselor effectiveness? Do client personality differences influence counselor behavior?

REFERENCES

1. Coleman, J.C. Psychology and Effective Behavior. Glenview, Illinois: Scott, Foresman, 1969, p. 161.

2. Lewis, E.C. The Psychology of Counseling. New York: Holt, Rinehart and Winston, 1970, pp. 110 - 111.

3. Rogers, C.R. On Becoming a Person. Boston: Houghton
    Mifflin, 1964, p. 34.

4. Yates, J.W. and Smith, L.D. "The Counselor's Self Concept,"
    Vocational Guidance Quarterly, 7 (Spring, 1959), 151.

5. Munson, H.L. Foundations of Developmental Guidance.
    Boston: Allyn and Bacon, 1971, pp. 120-121.

6. Benjamin, A. The Helping Interview. Boston: Houghton
    Mifflin, 1969, p. 46.

7. Shertzer, B. and Stone, S.C. Fundamentals of Counseling.
    Boston, Mass: Houghton Mifflin Co., 1968, pp. 348-349.

8. Nichols, R.G. and Stevens, L.A. Are You Listening?
    New York: McGraw-Hill, 1957, p. 45.

9. Atkin, J. "Counseling in an Age of Crisis," Personal
    and Guidance Journal, 50 (May, 1972), 723.

10. Berdie, R.F. "The 1980 Counselor: Applied Behavioral
    Scientist," Personal and Guidance Journal, 50,
    No. 6 (February, 1972), 451-456.

Chapter 3

THE COUNSELING PROCESS

Why People Seek Counseling

Prior to a detailed analysis of counseling techniques and practices, it would be beneficial to seek some answers to a vital question - why do people seek counseling? According to Lewis [1] people seek counseling for many reasons, but they would seem to have at least three characteristics in common:

1. The person is experiencing some sort of personal dissatisfaction. He is unable to behave in such a way as to reduce this dissatisfaction sufficiently. He thus perceives a need to change his behavior without knowing how to go about it.

2. The person approaches counseling with a substantial amount of anxiety and uncertainty. Not only is he troubled by some aspect of his life which he is handling inadequately, but he is taking a step into a strange and foreboding land: the counselor's office.

3. The person who seeks counseling expects that the counselor will be able to help him. . . The typical client, then, encounters counseling with an expectation that the counselor will help him deal more effectively with whatever is troubling him, but with no clear ideas as to just what will occur.

While the first two points made by Lewis might be frightening (especially to the beginning counselor), it should be remembered that an optimistic tone pervades the initial encounter - both counselor and client normally enter into the relationship with the expectation that its outcome will result in the behavior change agreed upon by both parties.

The Initial Interview

Most human interactions have a goal or purpose. So it is with the counseling relationship. The initial interview between counselor and client is significant in that it affords the first opportunity for these two people to embark upon a "relationship" within the context of the counseling relationship.

Munson [2] has suggested some assumptions that can be made about the process of counseling in the initial interview. It can be assumed (1) that the counselee wants or needs help; (2) that nothing specific needs to be accomplished beyond the structure required by the counselor; and (3) that the initial session is merely a stage - more frequently a beginning one - in a relationship between two individuals. Tyler [3] suggests three objectives for the counselor: (1) getting a sound counseling relationship started, (2) opening up the psychological realms of feelings and attitudes within the person, and (3) clarifying the structure of the helping process. Bucheimer and Balogh [4] divide the initial interview into three phases: (1) the statement of a problem, (2) exploration, and (3) closing and planning for the future. They are of the opinion that this represents a purposeful and goal-directed approach to counseling.

With the purpose and importance of the initial interview outlined above, it must be remembered that beginning interviewers, through lack of experience, usually commit many types of common errors. Emerick [5] has compiled a practical list of such common errors that the beginning counselor would seek to "avoid" during the interview or counseling session:

1. Avoid questions that may be answered simply "Yes" or "No." Try to frame the questions to elicit more complete responses. It is better to ask the parent, for instance, to tell you something about his child's behavior at home than to ask if the youngster gets along well with his brother or sister.

2. Avoid asking questions in such a way that their form inhibits freedom of response. Do not say, "You didn't have any difficulty with the child's toilet training, did you?" or, "You don't tell Billy to stop and start over again, do you?" Such leading questions are not effective in interviewing.

3. Avoid talking too much. It is much better to rephrase what the respondent has said or make some comment like "I see," "Tell me more," or "Anything else?"

4. Avoid concentrating on the physical symptoms and the etiological factors to the exclusion of the parent's feelings and attitudes. There is a little bit of Dr. Kildare in all of us; we yearn to play the role of physician.

5. Avoid providing information too soon. There will be plenty of time to clear up misconceptions later in the interview.

6. Avoid qualifying and hemming and hawing when asking questions. Ask them in a straightforward fashion, maintaining eye contact. Rather than asking, "Did you find that, well, you know, when you were, ah, shall we say 'with child' did you experience any untoward conditions?" say, "Did anything unusual happen during your pregnancy?"

7. Avoid negativistic or moralistic responses – verbal or nonverbal – to the parent's statements. The flow of information will stop rapidly and the relationship will be impaired severely if the parent senses that we find him or his behavior distasteful.

8. Avoid abrupt transitions in bringing the parent back to the point when he strays. The ability to make smooth transitions characterizes the experienced interviewer.

9. Avoid allowing the interview to produce only superficial or surface answers. We need ways to get deeper, more significant responses from parents.

10. Avoid letting the parent reveal too much in one interview. Sometimes a beginning interviewer makes the mistake of trying to get everything in one setting.

11. Avoid trusting to memory. Put the clinical situation, procedures, observations and recommendations in writing as soon as possible.

Structuring the Counseling Relationship

At the outset, many counselors will feel compelled to clarify or outline procedures that will be followed during the counseling relationship. It should be kept in mind, that hard-and-fast rules are difficult to state with accuracy because one counselor's theoretical frame of reference may differ markedly from another. While one counselor would prefer to present the approach he will take (the roles and functions of both parties), another counselor may wish to simply proceed with the task of relating, thereby leaving structuring (assuming it is necessary) to transpire at appropriate times during the course of the relationship.

If formal structuring is necessary, it is important to realize that the circumstances favor the counselee's acceptance of the counselor's approach. As mentioned earlier, the client is anxious and uncertain, and the counselor is in a favored position not only because of his confidence and calmness, but also because he has the status of an authority figure. Much of the counseling will be set in proper directions if the client has faith in the counselor and the approach they will take. This involves commitment on the part of the client and this is a vital step for it implies going beyond merely accepting the counselor's approach. This is not to suggest that the approach set forth by the counselor will always be easy for the client to accept. Much, of course, depends on the degree to which the approach meets the client's preconceived ideas of the counseling sessions and the role of each in the process. Should disagreement occur, a length of time for accommodation and further deliberations may be necessary.

One of the most vital transactions to occur during the initial session consists of the counselor and client agreeing on the procedure that will be followed and the role that each will follow during future meetings. This will be discussed later in more detail. Suffice it to say that at some point during the initial meetings, talk must be translated into a course of action toward the attainment of a counseling goal.

PHASES OF COUNSELING

Counseling Techniques and Practices

On the surface, or to the casual observer, counseling may appear to be a disorganized and haphazard process. For purposes of classification, counseling may be thought of as consisting of six developmental steps:

1. Determining the Concern for Consideration

This is also often referred to as the establishment of purpose. During this step, the client should indicate his reason for seeking counseling. This is important both from a motivational and directional viewpoint because it identifies a goal toward which both client and counselor may work. It is also during this phase that the counselor becomes an active listener and attempts to convey to the client that he values him as a person.

34

2. Defining the Counseling Process
        The counselor and counselee should agree as to
    how the mutually acceptable goal will be achieved. It
    is during this phase that the client needs assistance
    in developing some ideas as to the nature and function
    of counseling. Counselor and client, then, attempt
    to reach a mutual agreement as to the purpose and dir-
    ection of their relationship. It is during this phase
    that "rapport" is established. With the addition of
    trust and confidence conveyed between the two, a com-
    fortable communication of thoughts and feelings may be
    exchanged between counselor and client.

3. Understanding of Client's Needs
        The next step is to clarify the nature of the
    client's difficulty and to seek insight into the dyna-
    mics of the behavior. In this phase of the counseling
    process, the counselor is concerned with the client's
    perception of his difficulties and his feelings con-
    cerning them. The counselor and client, working to-
    gether, attempt to examine as many facets of the dif-
    ficulty as possible so that an appropriate plan of at-
    tack can be formulated.

        Understanding "alone" is not sufficient. The
    counselor must verbally express to the client his
    sense of understanding about him. It is during this
    phase that the construct of "empathy" assumes special
    significance - the ability to perceive the client's
    thoughts and feelings and to communicate this under-
    standing. Learning to develop empathy with the client
    takes both time and practice. It is learning to hear
    the client and to convey to him that you heard him.
    For example, if the client becomes tearful, the coun-
    selor would attempt to understand the feeling under-
    lying the tears and thereby help the client acknowledge
    and accept his feelings.

4. Exploring the Possible Alternatives or Plan to Follow
        Counselors have the responsibility to point out
    the many possible solutions and alternatives which ap-
    ply to the case at hand. This is to say that they
    should make progress toward the client's goal. It is
    not the counselor's duty to decide what decisions the
    counselee should make or to choose an alternative

course of action for him. In the final analysis decisions are, and rightfully should be, the counselee's own, and he must know why and how he made them. Furthermore, the counselee should learn to estimate the consequences of his actions in terms of personal effort, sacrifice, time, money, risk and other significant variables that may affect progress toward the ultimate goal.

5. Planning a Course of Action
   As the client becomes more aware of his thoughts and feelings, and with the assistance of the counselor in a supporting role, the client begins to move steadily toward his counseling goal. Executing a plan of action is normally much easier if the client has made the selection of his own plan of action. If a parent has decided on the course he is to take, we may expect a personal commitment and consquently a concentrated effort in carrying it out. The counselor must remember that the human personality varies considerably and should, therefore, not be disappointed if the desired ends (the counseling goals) are not fully attained as a result of counseling.

   What has been called the "progress" phase of counseling continues until the client and counselor agree that the counseling can and should be concluded. Agreement to terminate the sessions would indicate either that the goal has been reached or that the client feels that he is capable of continuing alone without further assistance. Prior to final termination, it is advisable to encourage the client to review his counseling experiences, especially in regard to probable future development. The rationale for this is to encourage the client to recognize and take advantage of insights gained about himself and seek to apply self-understanding toward future endeavors. The outcome of counseling should lead to a general improvement not only in the client's ability to cope with himself but also his ability to meet the situational demands of daily functioning.

6. Terminating the Counseling Session
   The final step in the counseling session is to terminate the interview. This may be considered from two points of view. First, it can be considered from a temporary point of view in which the client could continue his contacts at a later date with the counselor.

Second, consideration can be given to terminating the counseling session if the client feels that the counseling goal has been reached and there will be no need to continue the counseling relationship. In any event, the effects of the counseling session will hopefully continue beyond any final termination of the counseling sessions. The counseling session is best terminated on a positive note, so that if new difficulties arise the client may not feel the need for a counselor. In terminating counseling either temporarily or finally, it is very important that the parents depart with a feeling that something constructive has been accomplished. This feeling or positive attitude will normally prevail if an adequate job is done by the counselor; however, this feeling will be enhanced if the counselor is systematic and exercises tact and diplomacy in closing the counseling relationship.

In an ideal situation, the decision to terminate counseling should be a mutual one, although either party should feel free to discuss the possibility at any time during the counseling encounter. A good rule of thumb to follow is that the client is the master of his own fate and should assume the major responsibility for this decision as with all his decisions.

Using a slightly different order and emphasis, Brammer [6] lists eight stages in the helping process:

1. Entry: Preparing the helpee and opening the relationship.

2. Clarification: Stating the problem or concern and reasons for seeking help.

3. Structure: Formulating the contract and the structure.

4. Relationship: Building the helping relationship.

5. Exploration: Exploring problems, formulating goals, planning strageties, gathering facts, expressing deeper feelings, learning new skills.

6. Consolidation: Exploring alternatives, working through feeling, practicing new skills.

8. Planning: Developing a plan of action using strategies to resolve conflicts, reducing painful feelings,
   and consolidating and generalizing new skills or behaviors to continue self-directed activities.

9. Termination: Evaluating outcomes and terminating the
   relationship.

PROBLEMS FOR INDIVIDUAL STUDY AND CLASS DISCUSSION

1. Recall a time that you felt a need for counseling. Apply
   Lewis's three characteristics of why people seek counseling
   to your personal situation. Did you actually seek counseling?
   Why or why not? What was the outcome?

2. Do you think that a person having a personal, social or emotional problem is usually unwilling to approach a professional person for counseling? What factors might account
   for one's hesitancy in initiating a counseling relationship?

3. To what extent should the counselor expect to "fully" understand the client's needs? How much client understanding and
   awareness is necessary in order to proceed with the counseling
   relationship? To what degree might one expect this to develop
   during the counseling relationship?

4. Devise and structure a role playing situation in which "empathy" is conveyed and thereby developed and facilitated.
   Analyze the nature and flow of verbal communication as well
   as non-verbal actions which may be perceived as establishing
   empathy.

5. Devise and structure a role playing situation in which counseling is to be terminated - or termination is to be discussed.
   (Taping the session for replay may be helpful.) What considerations or factors arose which would be helpful for class
   analysis and discussion?

6. Is it correct to assume that most parents of exceptional children will cooperate readily if they sense you want to help
   their children? Should this be the dominant theme in your
   opening remarks? How might you convey this idea in genuine,
   constructive ways?

REFERENCES

1. Lewis, E.C. The Psychology of Counseling. New York:
   Holt, Rinehart and Winston, 1970, pp. 59-60.

2. Munson, H.L. Foundations of Developmental Guidance.
   Boston: Allyn and Bacon, 1971, pp. 133.

3. Tyler, L.E. The Work of the Counselor. New York:
   Appleton-Century-Crofts, 1969, p. 63.

4. Bucheimer, A. and Balogh, S.C. The Counseling Relationship.
   Chicago: Science Research Associates, 1961, p. 15.

5. Emerick, L. The Parent Interview. Danville, Illinois:
   Interstate Printers and Publishers, 1969, pp. 20-27.

6. Brammer, L.M. The Helping Relationship: Process and
   Skills. New Jersey: Prentice Hall, 1973, p. 55.

Chapter 4

APPROACHES IN COUNSELING

This chapter will explore four counseling approaches that should be understood by the counselor. The diverse points of view discussed in this chapter represent some of the fundamental counseling models that are characteristic of the helping relationship. Given this information, counselors are then in a better position to apply the appropriate approach to the various problem areas that will be encountered in the counseling process. Additional study, application, and discussion of these approaches is necessary in order to develop competencies in their use.

The Three Traditional Approaches

For many years, counseling has been heavily influenced by what the author refers to as the three traditional counseling approaches. (1) The directive or counselor-centered approach, (2) the non-directive or client-centered approach, and (3) the eclectic approach in counseling. These techniques will be briefly considered so as to illustrate the nature and function of each school of thought. The sophisticated counselor should also be aware of the basic concepts underlying these major counseling approaches.

The Directive Approach in Counseling

The directive approach is often referred to as the clinical or counselor-centered approach in counseling. The leading exponent of this school of thought is E.G. Williamson. In Williamson's viewpoint the overall goal of counseling is to facilitate the development of excellence in all aspects of human life.

The clinical viewpoint holds that the counselor actively influences the development of the client. Williamson [1] contends that the individual's freedom "to become" includes self-destructive and antisocial forms of individuality as well as positive development. According to Williamson, man has potentiality for either good or evil and the purpose of counseling is to assist in actualizing the "good" potential in man, particularly in the case of the client who lacks the environmental experiences necessary to foster his "good" drives and impulses.

If the client lacks certain environmental experiences, the counselor by virtue of his background and training should be equipped to understand the patient's concerns and lead him toward making a satisfactory adjustment to his situation. Because he is involved in analyzing, diagnosing, presenting information, clarifying issues, and the like, the counselor is active in the learning process of the client. However, the Williamsonian counselor must not be overly therapeutically ambitious and must be able to accept the fact that he will be of limited use to those parents whose problems are primarily long-term emotional reactions which are best solved by therapeutic help.

The work of the clinical counselor is divided into six steps by Williamson [2]. The first of these, "Analysis," involves collecting data from a wide variety of sources to obtain an understanding of the client. "Synthesis" follows with the summarizing and organizing of the data to determine the client's strengths and liabilities. "Diagnosis," the next step, is the counselor's conclusions about the causes and characteristics of the problem. "Prognosis" refers to the counselor's prediction of the diagnosis. "Counseling" means the steps taken by counselor and counselee with new or recurring problems as well as evaluation of the effectiveness of counseling. "Follow-up" is assisting with new problems.

A frequent criticism of the Williamson approach is that it over-emphasizes and over-values counselor control and that such emphasis often results in the counselee's becoming overly dependent upon the more mature counselor for direction and proper courses of action. Such a viewpoint makes a rigid interpretation of Williamson. In assisting a parent to achieve a satisfactory and effective adjustment to the concern he is experiencing, the counselor is not dictatorial. However, he does offer his experience and understanding as they relate to the parent's difficulty and does not hesitate to use his special skills in the giving of advice concerning decisions and proposing alternative courses of action. It should become obvious, however, that one major "disadvantage" of the counselor - centered approach is that adverse consequences may occur as the result of poor counselor judgment.

According to Porter [3], a major "advantage" of this method is that it usually requires only a limited number of interviews and therefore is more realistic in terms of the amount of time actually available in most schools and agencies. Furthermore, the active role of the counselor allows the client to benefit from the judgment and experience of a mature, trained, and experienced person that he can use as a "sounding board", for his thinking. Since this is the type of counseling help most people expect or anticipate when they enter a counseling relationship, the process can usually proceed with a minimum amount of structuring.

The Non-Directive or Client-Centered Approach

Non-directive counseling is often called self-theory counseling, client-centered counseling, or Rogerian counseling. The acknowledged leader of this school of thought is Carl Rogers, whose views have had a tremendous impact on the practice of counseling and psychotherapy in this country. His approach to counseling is based upon the humanistic belief that people's problems are primarily of an emotional etiology and that most clients already possess the objective information they need to make a decision about a problem.

Rogers has a deep and abiding faith in the goodness of man and in man's potential for positive growth, given the right kind of conditions. He argues that man has the basic capacity to set the correct goal and make correct choices if he is able to see his problems in an objective manner in a situation free from threat. This is why Rogers originally referred to this type of counseling as "non-directive" counseling, meaning that the counselor or therapist does not lead the client but stresses the counselee's ability both to determine the issues important to him and to solve his own problems.

In the Rogerian counseling process, the most significant aspect of the counseling relationship is the establishment of a warm, permissive, and accepting climate which permits the client to express his feelings and gain meaningful insights into his unique experience. The counselor provides a situation in which the parent may thoroughly discuss his concerns with one who is genuinely willing to listen. Once the counselor has established a relationship which is characterized by feelings of understanding, acceptance, lack of evaluation, and lack of threat, the client can, in turn, lower his self-defenses and begin to gain insight into his feelings, which enables him to express, examine, and incorporate previous experiences into his self-concept. Thus the counselor assists the parent in coming to a satisfactory conclusion in regard to his difficulty.

In order to be a success at client-centered counseling, the counselor must learn to share the individual's internal frame of reference, since, as Rogers says: "The best vantage point for understanding behavior is from the internal frame of reference of the individual himself." To do this the counselor must be able to convey to the client his attitude of genuine liking, his complete absence of value judgment, his total concentration on the client's problems, and finally, his ability to share this perceptual framework without losing his own identity. As Rogers [4] states:

> It is the counselor's function to assume insofar
> as he is able, the internal frame of reference of the
> client, to perceive the world as the client sees it,
> to lay aside all perceptions from the external frame
> of reference while doing so, and to communicate some-
> thing of this empathic understanding to the client.

From the discussion above, it can be seen that a crucial element in Rogerian counseling is the counselor's participation in the relationship as a genuine person. This process is facilitated by the skillful use of counseling techniques that include: (1) listening in-depth, (2) reflection of attitudes and feelings, and (3) clarification. Many of the counselor responses are open-ended or nonstructured leads which allow the client the opportunity to develop and understand his own problems and to express the emotional feelings of effect that accompanies them. Hackney and Nye [5] suggest that one of the better ways to help the client to identify and express feelings is for the counselor to model this process; this is, the counselor expresses a feeling about himself or about how he might feel if he were the client. The counselor might express his own feelings by saying: "I think we've really gotten somewhere today and I feel good about that." The counselor might also express how he would feel if he were in the client's situation by saying: "If she had treated me that way, I think I would have been pretty angry." This strategy is particularly helpful to the client who is unable, for whatever reason, to make appropriate emotional responses.

A major advantage of Rogerian counseling is that it does not reinforce client dependency by having the counselor make decisions for the client. Instead, it places responsibility on the client to find solutions to his problems within himself. The client, then, is the deciding agent of the counseling process.

Perhaps the major disadvantage of client-centered counseling is that the basic assumption of affective, emotional causation has the effect of making all clients fit the mold of having emotional problems regardless of what their own perception of their problems may be. Two other disadvantages may also be noted. The counselor is expected to be neutral, neither condemning nor condoning the actions or feelings of the client. Is it possible for any counselor to be valueless in an interpersonal situation? Finally, due to the techniques needed to effectively utilize Rogerian counseling, a series of interviews is usually required. Obviously, the process is often considered too time-consuming to be realistic.

The Eclectic Viewpoint

According to Hitchcock, [6] the eclectic approach in counseling is a point of view that looks on the method of counseling as not a "neither this nor that proposition," but as an approach where directive and non-directive techniques are employed to aid the client in his adjustment to life's problems. This approach is often referred to as the middle-of-the-road approach. Although there are many followers of this school of thought, possibly the person contributing most to eclecticism through his writing is Frederick Thorne. In his book, Principles of Personality Counseling, he discusses this approach of counseling in a systematic way. This position calls for a scientific study of all methods of diagnosis and treatment, and as Thorne [7] expresses it: "To the degree which eclecticism is able to integrate all operational methods and find ways available at time and place, it appears to us that it must represent the last word concerning what we can validly understand and apply in practice."

The eclectic model is based on two assumptions: (1) that people differ in their capacity to cope with life and its problems and therefore need different types of assistance; (2) that an adequate diagnosis is essential to any science which proposes to properly identify causes and then to select and administer appropriate methods of treatment.

According to Thorne [8], the process of personality counseling involves the following stages:

1. diagnosis of the cause of personality maladjustments

2. making a plan for modifying etiologic factors

3. securing proper conditions for efficient learning

4. stimulating the client to develop his own resources and assume responsibility for practicing new modes of adjustment

5. proper handling of any related problems which may contribute to adjustment

The eclectic counseling relationship is characterized by warmth, understanding, and acceptance. In addition, emphasis is placed on reassurance and information-giving in order to facilitate and promote client learning. Any counselor who seeks to operate effectively from an "eclectic" framework should hold to a scientific view of man, be well-versed in broad diagnostic skills, and have an openness which allows flexibility of style and technique.

One major advantage of eclecticism is that Thorne has analyzed the best aspects of other approaches and applied them "scientifically" into an integrated system retaining the best features of each. This diversity and flexibility of technique would normally permit the counselor to work with a more diverse clientele.

A common criticism of the eclectic approach is that it is not realistic in terms of most of counselor's achieving expertise in a multiplicity of counseling methods and styles. Counselors have an ingrained tendency to develop a style suitable to their personality and often sacrifice effectiveness when they try to adapt to another technique. Furthermore, it is not realistic to believe that most counselors have had the academic and diagnostic training necessary for proficiency in this type of counseling.

The Action or Behavioral Approach

Only in recent years have counselors begun to respond to the challenge presented in 1962 by Michael and Meyerson in their article, "A Behavioral Approach to Counseling and Guidance." In this provocative article they state that "Observable behavior is the only variable of importance in the counseling and guidance process, and it is the only criterion against which the outcome of the process can be evaluated." Taking the basic premise of B.F. Skinner's operant learning, they further point out that "Behavior is controlled by its environmental consequences and an effective procedure for producing behavioral change is the manipulation of the environment so as to create consequences that will produce the desired behavior" [9]. Counselors who adopt the behavioral approach would obviously define behavior as the interaction between heredity and environment. Thus, this kind of counseling is a process involving a learning situation, in which the counselee learns more appropriate behaviors, and counselors who favor this approach lean heavily on theories of learning as a guide for their counseling interviews. Another basic premise held by the behavioral counselor is that if most human behavior is learned, it can be unlearned or relearned. Human behavior is, therefore not static, fixed, or predetermined, but subject to change.

From the behavioral point of view, the most significant aspect of the counseling relationship is to structure the situation so as to optimize observable changes in client behavior once the desired behaviors have been specified. For example, whereas the non-directive counselor might suggest a counseling goal such as "to improve the client's self-concept," the behavior oriented counselor would specify those behaviors which would lead to new ways of coping with his problems and thereby indicating an improved self-concept. Ullman and Krasner [10] suggest three major initial questions that the behavioral counselor is likely to ask:

1. "What behavior is maladaptive; that is, what subject behaviors should be increased or decreased?"

2. "What environmental contingencies currently support the subject's behavior?"

3. "What environmental changes, usually reinforcing stimuli, may be manipulated to alter the subject behavior?"

46

Dustin and George [11] describe action or behavioral counseling as consisting of three essential phases. In Phase I, the counselor begins his contacts with the client by listening and communicating empathic understanding in order to develop a special kind of relationship. Phase II is the stage in which counselor and client decide which of the various avenues to take in order to meet the client's needs and to determine those techniques that will be most effective in helping the client get there. In Phase III, the client follows an action plan, and more and more of the conversation between the counselor and client is based on what the client did, what he would like to do, and together, what they can do to bring about the client's objectives. According to this viewpoint, three phases of counseling-relationship, choice, and action - are joined to provide a meaningful, effective approach toward behavior change.

A major advantage of behavioral counseling is that it should be a useful supplementary technique to allow an in-depth approach which stresses observable behavioral changes. The behavioral approach is also advantageous from a motivational viewpoint in that those who begin to see changes occur are reinforced in their efforts to continue the change process. One disadvantage should be obvious. Unfortunately, most counselors and those who aspire to be effective counselors have had only a superficial introduction to a few behavior theories and know little if anything about such theories. A counselor who adopts a behavioral approach should, without question, be well-versed in learning theory in order to provide experiences that will facilitate individual development most efficiently.

This chapter has explored four approaches that counselors may use in helping their clients toward self-fulfillment. It must be remembered that how people behave and act at every moment of their lives is determined by the basic need of the human organism for personal realization. There is, however, another vital question which needs attention - what factors affect the counselor's approach? Obviously, there are many factors which will help determine the counselor's approach and course of action. A listing of some of the major considerations is as follows:

1. the counselor's philosophy of counseling

2. the counselor's concept of the role he is to play

3. the competencies and experience of the counselor

4. the particular concern of the parent (parents present different kinds of problems and need different kinds of help)

5. the parent's being capable of assuming his role in the counseling process

While consideration of these factors may be helpful, the question of exactly what technique or techniques to be used when attempting to motivate and counsel the parent of an exceptional child remains relatively unanswered.

PROBLEMS FOR INDIVIDUAL STUDY AND CLASS DISCUSSION

1. What individual variables can you cite as possible influences on the approach one will take in a counseling situation?

2. Which of the four approaches mentioned in this chapter do you feel would present the most difficulty for the person without formal training in counseling? Why?

3. What type of counseling approach would appear to work best with individuals faced with a choice situation where they need information, understanding, emotional support and acceptance in order to make the correct decision?

4. Have two people representing a client and counselor define a problem and role-play a counseling session employing a particular counseling approach. See if the class can identify which approach was used by analyzing the exchange between client and counselor.

5. Complete this statement: A counselors approach to counseling is governed in part by his _____.
Compare your response with others in the class or with another person.

6. Of the counseling approaches discussed, which one would you judge to be the most systematic? Why?

7. Of the counseling approaches discussed, which one would you judge to be the most valid on a scientific basis? Why?

8. Do you agree with Carl Rogers' belief that people's problems are primarily of an emotional etiology and that most clients already possess the objective information that they need to make a decision about a problem? Now substitute the words, "parents of exceptional children" for "clients." Has your opinion changed?

9. Which of the approaches discussed would probably work best with individuals who, by nature, are timid and reserved and quite fearful of seeking help or becoming actively involved in a counseling relationship? Why?

10. How valid is this statement: It is impossible for a counselor to provide the correct form of counseling service (treatment) without first identifying what it is that the client needs (diagnosis).

11. Should the beginning teacher/counselor experiment with the different types of counseling approaches or be content to use the one with which he feels most comfortable? What are some advantages and disadvantages of experimentation with counseling approaches?

12. Do you agree or disagree that giving advice is a purposeful counseling activity because it is a time-honored function of any relationship in which trust and understanding are present?

13. Once counseling decisions are made, what factors influence their implementation?

14. List specific ways in which plans, decisions, and behavioral operations may be evaluated?

15. Do you agree or disagree that, in essence, the counselor of parents of exceptional children is dealing with problems of human behavior and, therefore, is essentially working with the fundamentals of psychology? What implications does this have?

REFERENCES

1. Williamson, E.G. "Some Issues Underlying Counseling Theory and Practice," in Counseling Points of View, ed., Willis E. Dugan. Minneapolis: University of Minnesota Press, 1959, p. 3.

2. Williamson, E.G., quoted in Shertzer, B. & Stone, S.C.
    Fundamentals of Counseling, New York: Houghton Mifflin,
    1968, p. 250.

3. McGowan, J.F. & Porter, T.L. An Introduction to the Vocational
    Rehabilitation Process. U.S. Department of Health,
    Education, and Welfare, 1967, p. 112.

4. Rogers, C.R. Client Centered Therapy. Boston: Houghton
    Mifflin, 1951, p. 29.

5. Hackney, H. and Nye, S. Counseling Strageties and Objectives.
    New Jersey: Prentice-Hall, 1973, p. 104.

6. Hitchcock, W.L. The Counseling Service. Georgia State
    Department of Education, 1964, p. 22.

7. Thorne, F.C. "Clinical Judgement," Journal of Clinical
    Psychology, (1961), p. 240.

8. Thorne, F. C. "Principles of Personality Counseling,"
    Journal of Clinical Psychology, (1950), 88-89.

9. Michael, J. and Meyerson, L. "A Behavioral Approach to
    Counseling and Guidance," Harvard Educational
    Review, 32 (1962), 395-396.

10. Ullmann, L.P., and Krasner, L. Case Studies in Behavior
    Modification. New York: Holt, Rinehart and Winston,
    1965.

11. Dustin, R. and George, R. Action Counseling for Behavior
    Change. New York: Intext Educational Publishers, 1973.

Chapter 5

SPECIAL TOPICS/PROBLEMS IN THE COUNSELING PROCESS

This section will complete the first part of this text by identifying and discussing some of the significant topics and problems that inevitably occur during the counseling process. Hopefully, an in-depth understanding and awareness of these topics will allow the counselor to assume a more effective and professional role in helping the parents of exceptional children make a better adjustment to their problems and concerns.

Group Counseling

The development of group counseling has a short history of thirty to forty years. Although it was slow gaining acceptance, such counseling has expanded rapidly during the last decade in both school and nonschool settings. This growth has led some to have concerns with its effectiveness. Mahler [1], for example, says that "it appears that our favorite child, group counseling, has attained the adolescent stage of development, with all the anxiety and confusion accompanying it. One major concern is the too frequent naive view that the mere placing of individuals in a group will be good for them." This holds that anyone versed in the fundamentals of individual counseling should be able to effectively conduct group counseling.

In spite of such criticism, a teacher or counselor should be skilled in working with groups of parents should the need arise. In the group counseling situation, one counselor is involved in a meaningful relationship with a number of counselees at the same time. Group counseling may be defined as a social experience which is usually concerned with developmental problems and the situational concerns of members. Cohn and his associates [2] offer the following definition: "Group counseling as we see it, is a dynamic. interpersonal process through which individuals with a normal range of adjustment work within a peer group and with a professionally trained counselor, exploring problems and feelings in an attempt to modify their attitudes so that they are better able to deal with developmental problems."

According to Lewis [3] the most acceptable objective of group counseling lies in the positive use which can be made of the group situation to help the individual members reach their counseling goals. If conducted properly, group counseling should provide the individual members with an opportunity to interact with others who are striving to reach similar counseling goals and to give and accept help from them as well as from the counselor. Group counseling certainly helps to demonstrate that others have similar difficulties and problems. The group format also often helps the nonverbal client or the person who cannot adequately cope with threatening situations.

In the group situation, the role of the counselor is basically the same as in one-to-one counseling: to provide a relationship in which the client can feel free to express his thoughts and feelings. It is important the client feels he is being understood. This necessitates that the counselor and other group members must learn to listen perceptively and with understanding. The counselor should always remember that in group counseling, the topic is derived from the immediate or stated concerns of the group members.

Much discussion has revolved around the question – what is the optimum size of a group? Most authorities suggest six or seven as an optimum number, with a range from five to ten. As a general rule, the group should be small enough so that a meaningful interaction can transpire through the sharing of personal concerns with one's peers and the counselor. By the same token, the group should be large enough to stimulate group interaction and self-expression. There is also the possibility that a group which is too small may be dominated by one particular member.

While group counseling has its disadvantages and one of the greatest is the demand it places on the skills and competencies of the counselor, it can be an effective tool for working with parents, especially if the counselor's time is too limited for individual sessions. It can allow group members to develop rapport, to trust each other and thereby share not only information but also personal thoughts and feelings.

Ethical Considerations

Imposing on the role and function of the helping person or counselor are a number of ethical considerations. In a thought provoking article Schwebel [4] suggests that unethical behavior –

may occur for any of three reasons: (1) the counselor behaves out of ignorance, (2) the counselor does not have sufficient training, or (3) the counselor acts out of self-interest. In view of these possibilities, the client should be protected from possible harm by persons who act in an unprofessional manner.

In order to determine if a behavior is or is not unethical, any profession needs to formulate general guidelines to assist the practitioner in his daily activities. An important source of such guidance is the code of ethics of a profession. To be meaningful, a code of ethics should reflect not only the agreed-upon values of the profession represented but also values generally accepted by the society the profession serves. Before a group can state an ethical code, it must first seek out commonly agreed-upon underlying values and responsibilities. After a series of such attempts at definition of basic values, the American Personnel and Guidance Association published in October, 1961, its adopted code of ethics [5]. Some of the major points in this code of ethics are as follows:

1. The members primary obligation is to respect the integrity and promote the welfare of the counselee or client with whom he is working.

2. The counseling relationship and information resulting therefrom must be kept confidential, consistent with the obligations of the member as a professional person.

3. The counselee or client should be informed of the conditions under which he may receive counseling assistance at or before the time he enters the counseling relationship.

4. The member shall decline to initiate or shall terminate a counseling relationship when he cannot be of professional assistance to the counselee or client either because of lack of competence or personal limitation.

While a code of ethics has no legal force, it serves a distinct purpose by offering general guidelines which normally enable an organization to suspend a member for a violation. An ethics code will not always, however, allow a person to resolve the counseling dilemmas that are encountered, for most ethical problems lie in a gray area between behavior that is or is not ethical. Professional, intelligent judgment is the key.

53

One of the major areas of ethical concern is the counselor's obligation to maintain confidentiality. Once a trust is violated by a counselor who talks freely and openly about his clients, it is difficult, if not impossible, to regain. There will be several situations in which answers regarding confidentiality will be difficult, especially for the beginning counselor. Schneiders [6] has suggested that the counselor's obligation to maintain confidentiality varies with both the nature of the information imparted and the effect that revelation would have upon the client. The author's opinion and suggestion is that when in doubt, always ask for the client's permission. The principle which stands out here is that information given by the client within a counseling relationship belongs to him unless released by him for other use.

The Physical Setting

The client's first impressions of counseling are obtained not only from the conduct of the counselor but also from the setting which has some bearing on whether the relationship will be facilitated or thwarted. One of the first concerns of the person who seeks to counsel others is to provide for privacy. No office, room, or area can lend itself to effective counseling if conversations can be easily overheard and distractions are frequent. The beginning counselor is encouraged to give careful thought to the physical setting as nothing can limit the relationship more quickly than the client's awareness that others are able to hear what is being said or watch what is taking place. The room or counseling area should also be comfortable and attractive. It should be of such a type and so furnished as to produce or convey a relaxed and intimate atmosphere. The arrangement of chairs is significant. If a desk is between them, this conveys a different relationship than if no barriers stand between counselor and client. For example, the non-directive counselor would avoid the authoritative position of sitting behind a desk and directly facing the client. The beginning counselor should experiment with various physical arrangements. In this way he will come to prefer the one in which he feels most relaxed and, more importantly, one which seems to him to communicate the type of relationship he hopes to establish and maintain with his client.

Silence in Counseling

As Shertzer and Stone [7] suggest, silence is difficult to master as a technique for most counselors who have been teachers. They often believe that client silence is synonymous with counselor failure and become uncomfortable when it occurs. Because silence in social situations tends to be looked upon as rejection, defiance, or disapproval, this meaning, from a different context, is quite often transferred to the counseling relationship. When pauses occur, the counselor may be overcome with the desire to break the silence rather than tolerate it. The counselor should always be aware that a great deal of communication takes place without sound.

The underlying principle of a successful conference requires both listening and talking, and the most common error made by beginning counselors is that they talk too much. My personal experience has been that most beginning interviewers find silence difficult to bear. A thirty-second period of silence will seem to last for a much longer duration and oftentimes be painful to endure. Thus, excessive amounts of verbiage by the counselor may, in fact, be an unconscious way of seeking to prevent these periods of silence from occurring. In time and with experience and confidence the counselor should learn to differentiate between silences and to appreciate and react to them differently.

Periods of silence can serve a useful purpose and actually enhance the helping relationship. There is, according to Benjamin [8], the silence the interviewee may require to sort out his thoughts and feelings. Silence of this sort can be most helpful if the interviewer does not feel threatened by it or uncomfortable with it, but can handle it with ease as part of an on-going process. Respect for this silence is more beneficial than many words from the interviewer. When ready, the interviewee will continue, usually quite soon - in a minute or so. The time will seem quite long at first, but with experience the counselor will learn to measure time internally. Should the silence endure, he may want to interject a brief remark to help the counselee go on; one can get lost in silence and generally appreciates the indication of a way out. For example, the counselor might say, "There must be lots going on within; I wonder if you are ready to share some of it with me."

There are several logical reasons why silence may occur: (1) the person being counseled may be the "naturally quiet" type and have difficulty expressing himself, (2) silence may occur because either counselor or client has reached the conclusion of an idea and does not know what to say next; (3) silence may indicate that the client is experiencing emotions which he has difficulty expressing, yet would like to do so, (4) a pause may mean that the client seeks assurance and support from the counselor, and (5) silence may be the result of a heavily emotional expression by the client.

There is no one standard rule for determining whether the counselor should remain silent or interrupt a period of silence. As stated earlier, sensitivity to silence and judgment about if and when to interrupt normally comes with experience. Above all, one should remember that silence does not necessarily indicate a halt in the counseling process. More than likely it indicates a period in which the client is thinking about himself or experiencing feelings and emotions of which he has just become aware.

It is often difficult to determine the meaning and cause of silence. The counselor should take moments of silence in stride and seek to convey to the client that silence is both expected and acceptable.

Nonverbal Communication: Meaning Beyond Words

Dr. Fredrick Perls, a leading Gestalt Psychologist, has stated, "Verbal communication is a lie. The real communication is beyond words." Similarly, the French writer Victor Hugo said, "When a woman is speaking to you, listen to what she says with her eyes." Victor Hugo was talking about what is now labeled "nonverbal communication." Body talk,- nonverbal communication - has gotten a good deal of clinical and popular attention in the past few years. This form of talk can be eloquent indeed in its capacity to confirm or contradict one's spoken words, for when people talk, the words they utter are only a part of their effort to communicate.

Nichols and Stevens [9], have observed, "the pitch and timbre of a person's voice; the way he pauses between words; the rhythm with which the words flow from his mouth; oddities in pronunciation; the speed at which words are spoken - all of these things have something to say, over and above that which is being communicated by words alone." An excellent example they give is the simple word "oh" which says little as you see it in printed form. But in spoken form, "oh" can acquire scores of meanings. According to the way in which it is

spoken, "oh" can mean: "You surprised me"; or "I made a mistake"; or "You're a pain in the neck"; or "You make me so
happy"; or "I'm bored"; or I'm fascinated"; or "I understand";
or "I don't understand."

    As you can see from this simple example, the nonverbal
messages that we receive as listeners reinforce, modify
or even contradict the words that a person speaks. Sometimes
the nonverbal part of the communication received by the listener is far more important than the verbal part. For example,
the counselor who can detect facial changes in emotion should
be in a better position to lead the interview in the appropriate direction.

    Hackney and Nye [10] suggest that nonverbal communication
may help the counselor interpret client silence. By watching
the client, he will be able to gather some clues to what is
happening. Is the client relaxed? Are his eyes fixed upon
something without being focused? A fixed stare usually means
he is thinking about something, examining a new idea, or rumi-
nating around in his mind. Is the client tense, appearing
nervous, looking from one object to another and avoiding eye
contact with you? This may mean that he is avoiding some
topic or idea. It can readily be seen that much of what
transpires between counselor and clients will be dependent
upon the nonverbal aspects of the relationship they engage in.

    The counselor should have a working knowledge of nonverbal
communication so that he can perceive the myraid of messages
that come to him from his client by this avenue, and be aware
of the messages of understanding and support, or lack thereof
that he is sending out to his client via this same route [11].
Nonverbal communication can no longer be ignored as a force
in shaping our understanding of another person.

The Referral Process

    By definition, referral is the act of transferring the cli-
ent to another person or agency for the purpose of specialized
assistance. A counselor who holds high ethical standards will
never attempt to undertake an activity which is outside of his
competency. The American Personnel and Guidance Association's -
ethical standard in respect to referral is as follows:

The member shall decline to initiate or shall terminate a counseling relationship when he cannot be of professional assistance to the counselee or client either because of lack of competency or personal limitation. In such instances, the member shall refer his counselee or client to an appropriate specialist. [12]

If in the counselor's opinion, referral seems a proper course of action, it is wise to discuss this with the client. The counselor, of course, must be fully familiar with the nature and scope of referral services and agencies prior to suggesting referral. Two important questions should guide him in his course of action - What kind of special service is required? Is this service available and if so, where? In sharing this information with the client, he should be tactful, yet straightforward and to the point. Although the client may become apprehensive or somewhat fearful at this point, the counselor's offer to arrange for the needed service rather than continue in an ineffective relationship should assure him of the counselor's acceptance and willingness to help. If the client is master of his own fate, he will then decide what further action to take. It is important, that the client understand the referral agency, its limitations and strengths, and the counselor should be particularly careful in communicating this information to the client and others involved with the client.

Parents As Behavior Modifiers

Parents have generally been cast in the role as receivers of information and advice from experts. Professionals involved in parent intervention programs now realize that parents make a unique contribution to the development of their children. Those who counsel with parents of exceptional children must look upon parents as active partners in the educational enterprise. Given instructions and encouragement, parents are capable of bringing about specified changes in their child's behavior. Don't forget that parents must be reinforced systematically for maintaining contingencies on the child.

Karnes and Zehrback [13] offered the opinion that one of the most important changes in programs for parents stems from the work of the behavior modification groups who have developed a variety of related procedures for helping parents learn how to make specific changes in their own and their child's behaviors.

The basic thrust of this approach requires the parent to specify exactly which child behaviors are his concern, gather data to record the frequency of such behavior, develop a specific procedure for changing the child's behavior, and then note the degree of change in the child's behavior. Implementation of this procedure requires that the teacher first learn the new techniques. Then the teacher must train the parent to use the techniques. This technique typically requires rewarding the child's positive behavior and ignoring his negative behavior. Rewards can take variety of forms from M & M's to verbal praise, from listening to records to trips to the beach.

Parents who can profit most from this approach are those who are fairly stable, can be consistent, and have a strong need to bring about positive change in their child's behavior. Further, the behavior that needs to be changed will likely occur with reasonable frequency.

An advantage of this approach is that it is flexible enough to be used in the classroom, at home, or in the community. Once the parent has learned the approach and is convinced that it can be used successfully, it can then be used to modify or change other behaviors of the child. One disadvantage of this approach is that initially parents find it hard to reward the positive behavior and ignore the negative behavior they wish to extinguish. Parents tend to be reluctant to believe the approach will work. In addition, ignoring a selected behavior of a child in the home may create problems for the other family members. A further disadvantage is that misapplication can lead to negative results just as appropriate application can lead to positive results.

Practical Suggestions for Effective Parent Counseling

The following suggestions are offered to the reader for one explicit purpose - to define and stress those practical, common sense factors and considerations which should help improve interpersonal relationships and thereby lead to more effective parent counseling. These are the obvious things we tend to forget or overlook, yet those which can be far - reaching and beneficial.

1. DECIDE IN ADVANCE WHAT IS TO BE DISCUSSED DURING THE PARENT CONFERENCE

Assemble a folder of the student's work and jot down a checklist of the various problems to talk about.

2. UNLESS YOU ASK FOR PERMISSION OR EXPLAIN YOUR PURPOSE, DON'T TAKE NOTES WHILE TALKING WITH PARENTS

They may feel intimidated and afraid to speak.

3. BEGIN AND END THE CONFERENCE WITH A POSITIVE AND ENCOURAGING COMMENT ABOUT THE CHILD

Many parents report they have never been contacted by a teacher or counselor except for negative information.

4. DON'T RUSH THE INTERVIEW

It will probably take time for parents to relax, tell what they are really worried about, and express their real feelings and fears.

5. LISTEN WITH ENTHUSIASM

Parents should be encouraged to do the talking, telling, and suggestion making. Give parents a chance to "sound off," especially when they are upset or angry. After they have let off steam, you will find it easier to discuss the problem calmly. Control your facial expressions of disapproval or anger.

6. BE WILLING TO AGREE WITH PARENTS WHENEVER POSSIBLE

When the answer must be "no," take your time in saying it softly, without a trace of hostility. Communication becomes impossible in the midst of anger and recrimination.

7. EXPLAIN SO THAT OTHERS CAN UNDERSTAND

Though this sounds obvious, all too often when dealing with parents, we assume understanding where it does not exist. Remember that obvious things are often the most difficult to perceive.

8. USE THE SIMPLEST AND CLEAREST WORDS YOU FIND TO EXPLAIN WHAT YOU AND THEIR CHILD DO IN SCHOOL

Gear your talk to the parents interests and don't talk down to parents. They are not children and resent being treated as such. Whether well-educated or not, a parent may be embarrassed to admit not knowing a term the counselor uses so familiarly such as speaking glibly of "behavioral objectives."

9. EXAMINE YOUR OWN EMOTIONAL REACTION TO CRITICISM

Do you dislike or feel threatened by people who give you new ideas, or who disagree with you? If so, you may be getting this message across in subtle, unspoken ways.

10. DON'T LET COMMENTS ABOUT OTHER CHILDREN CREEP INTO THE CONVERSATION

Avoid making comparisons with the child's brothers and sisters or members of his peer group.

11. PROVIDE THE PARENTS WITH AT LEAST ONE ACTION STEP - ONE THING THEY CAN DO AT HOME TO HELP THEIR CHILD OVERCOME A PARTICULAR PROBLEM YOU'VE BEEN DISCUSSING

Help them understand that their child's success in school must be a joint project of home and school. Action often minimizes the hopeless-helpless feeling of futility and anxiety.

12. AT THE CLOSE OF A CONFERENCE SUMMARIZE AND JOINTLY PLAN FOR THE NEXT CONFERENCE

The parent should feel at the close of the conference that something specific was accomplished and that future plans have been established.

13. DON'T FORGET THE FOLLOW-UP

The first step is to write down the gist of what was discussed. These notes should be carefully reviewed and considered when planning the next conference.

PROBLEMS FOR INDIVIDUAL STUDY AND CLASS DISCUSSION

1. Compare and contrast individual counseling with group counseling. Explain and discuss the similarities and differences.

2. Is it possible that a person could be skilled, effective individual counselor and somehow fail to work effectively with groups? If so, what are some reasons that might account for this?

3. Is it unethical to discuss a client with another professional person? What guidelines might you suggest for conduct in this area?

4. How should the counselor handle requests for information or impressions from persons who have other relationships with the client, for example, a parent or teacher?

5. As a means of testing one's toleration for silence, three persons can do this exercise. One person is the talker, one the listener, and the third person can be the timekeeper. The talker may talk about anything he wishes. The listener must wait 30 seconds between each response. The timer will signal when 30 seconds have expired. As this becomes a tolerable limit of time, gradually increase the "silent" time to 40 seconds, 50 seconds, etc. When the listener can tolerate silence for about two or three minutes without discomfort, exchange roles and repeat the exercise.

6. Arrange to role-play or video tape a hypothetical counseling session. Keep a log of specific instances of non-verbal communication such as a raised eyebrow, facial expressions, posture, gestures, mannerisms of a glance or look, intensity or increasing loudness or softness of the voice, raising or lowering of voice pitch and increased or decreased voice tempo. At the end of the session, compare your tally of non-verbal communications with another person and discuss possible inferences and implications.

7. What steps would you take to make a survey of referral agencies in your community? Compile a list of referral agencies in your community/city which offer services to parents of exceptional children. Include important data such as purpose of agency, eligibility criteria, nature of service, etc. Are there local civic clubs which do or would render services to the exceptional child?

8. Think of additional ways other than acting as "behavior modifiers" that parents can use to help bring about a change in the child behavior. Consider such examples as modeling, and the use of behavioral contracts.

9. What factors make for school-community solidarity and cooperation today? What factors operate against it, and why?

10. Explain your reasons for agreeing or disagreeing with this statement: There is not a great deal the teacher/counselor can do about the home situation except to be cognizant of it.

11. Every counselor should have some knowledge of what the lawyer calls "priviledged communication," so that if the situation arises, he may be able more readily to react and respond intelligently. What is privileged communication? Give specific examples of how this may be related to the counseling process.

REFERENCES

1. Mahler, C.A. "Group Counseling," Personnel and Guidance Journal, 49 (1971), 601.

2. Cohn, B., Combs, C.F., Gibian, E.J., and Sniffen, A.M. "Group Counseling: An Orientation," Personnel and Guidance Journal, 42 (1963), 355-356.

3. Lewis, E.C. The Psychology of Counseling. New York: Holt, Rinehart and Winston, 1970, p. 117.

4. Schwebel, M. "Why Unethical Practice?" Journal of Counseling Psychology, 2 (1955), 122-128.

5. Peterson, J.A. Counseling and Values. Scranton, Penn.: International Textbook, 1970, p. 120.

6. Schneiders, A.A. "The Limits of Confidentiality," Personnel and Guidance Journal, 42 (1963), 252.

7. Shertzer, B. & Stone, S.C. Fundamentals of Guidance. New York: Houghton Mifflin, 1968, p. 373.

8. Benjamin, A. The Helping Interview. Boston: Houghton Mifflin, 1969, pp. 25-26.

9. Nichols, R.G. & Stevens, L.A. Are You Listening? New York: McGraw-Hill, 1957, pp. 59-61.

10. Hackney, H. & Nye, S. Counseling Strategies and Objectives. Englewood Cliffs, New Jersey: Prentice-Hall, 1973, p. 24.

11. Hansen, J.C., Stevic, R.R., & Warner, R.W. <u>Counseling:</u>
     <u>Theory and Process</u>. Boston, Mass.: Allyn   and
     Bacon, 1972, p. 262.

12. "Ethical Standards," <u>Personnel and Guidance Journal</u>, 40
     (October, 1961), 207.

13. Karnes, M.B. and Zehrback, R.R. "Flexibility in Getting
     Parents Involved in the School," <u>Teaching Exceptional</u>
     <u>Children</u> (Fall, 1972), 14.

PART TWO

COUNSELING PARENTS OF EXCEPTIONAL CHILDREN

Introduction to Part II

This section will consist of a brief overview of some of the major problems, frustrations, and rewards that accompany parents of exceptional children. Since it would take a multi-volume work to fully explore this broad and diverse topic, the author's primary goal is to raise some basic issues, indicate appropriate research findings, and provoke the reader to pursue additional study in areas of personal interest. The questions for study at the end of each chapter should identify and raise additional issues for individual and/or group study. It is hoped that a perusal of the chapters in this section will aid the professional - regardless of his or her level of competence and experience - in better preparing for effective counseling relationships with parents of the exceptional child.

Chapter 6

COUNSELING PARENTS OF THE MENTALLY HANDICAPPED CHILD

In the professional literature treating exceptional children, the most extensive studies have dwelt with the etiology, nature, and characteristics of the mentally handicapped. Yet, for the layman or professional, the comprehension of mental deficiency is in many respects more perplexing than other types of handicaps. Ross [1] gives the following illustration:

Even though the sighted person cannot possibly know how it feels like to be blind he can nevertheless imagine what it is like by walking blindfolded into a strange room. He can similarly imagine what it is like to be deaf or otherwise physically impaired. On the other hand, it is totally impossible to achieve any degree of empathy for the state of the mental defective for we cannot suspend our higher mental processes or temporarily cancel everything we learned.

This, then becomes one of the counselor's major tasks - to help the parents understand the basic nature of their child's condition. Once this is accomplished, the counselor can seek to influence the behavior and attitude of the parents.

Parental Reaction

The first severe problem which parents of retarded children face is the acceptance of the fact that the child is intellectually retarded. Such acceptance is indeed a difficult task, especially in our present-day society where a great premium is set on educational success and intellectual attainment. Mental retardation is perhaps even more difficult for a family with high intellectual standards and expectations. As a result, this situation, in itself, may produce various emotional and psychological problems such as worries, anxieties, anger and excessive guilt. The counselor's consideration must be aimed at the attitudes and feelings of the parents. The counselor must not only dispense factual information, but actively assist the parents to learn to work with the child as he is.

Upon learning that they have a retarded child, parents may also feel that they are uniquely alone and isolated. Perhaps one of the greatest needs of parents is to have someone with whom they can talk, someone who will understand their feelings, someone who can share their fears and concerns and someone with expertise in the field of retardation. Do you fit this description? If so, that someone can be you!

The Diagnosis

In a real sense, the parents' most critical hour of need is at the time the diagnosis is first presented. At this time most parents are usually unable to face their problems realistically and resolve them constructively. They especially need help in handling their emotions and assistance in planning for the child. The typical process of counseling parents involves providing support so that they can go beyond their present level of understanding to some realistic, positive level. The counselor must be able to judge this present level before he can assess the degree of change needed and determine a proper course of direction. Stone [2] has suggested some ways of judging parental awareness:

Considerable Awareness

1. The parent states that the child is retarded.

2. The parent recognizes the limitations of any treatment.

3. The parent requests information about suitable care and training.

Partial Awareness

1. The parent describes the symptoms of retardation with questions about the causes.

2. The parent hopes for improvement but fears that treatment will not be successful.

3. The parent questions his own ability to cope with the problems.

4. The worker evaluates him as having partial awareness of the child's real problem.

1. The parent refuses to recognize that certain characteristic behavior is abnormal.

2. The parent blames causes other than retardation for the symptoms.

3. The parent believes that treatment will produce a normal child.

Parents Have Questions

After the diagnosis is completed, many questions arise when parents seek further help. Two authors [3] have gone so far as to compile a list of 231 fundamental questions and answers. A sample of these questions is provided below although not necessarily listed in order or degree because this will usually depend upon the family setting, the nature of the child's defect, and the parents' level of sophistication.

1. What is the cause of our child's retardation?

2. How severely retarded is he (she)?

3. Why did this have to happen to us?

4. Is it safe to have another child?

5. Does the genetic background of one parent contribute more to the retardation of a child than that of the other parent?

6. Can mental retardation be "cured"?

7. Can mental retardation be prevented?

8. I cannot help but pity my child. Is this wrong?

9. If our retarded child lives at home, will it affect our normal child adversely?

10. How shall we explain him (or her) to our normal children?

11. How shall we explain him (or her) to our relatives, friends, and neighbors?

12. Should we belong to a parent organization?
    What are the advantages of belonging to a
    parent group?

General Counseling Goals

In addition to dispensing factual information which may
need to be repeated and reviewed at different times and in
different contexts, the competent counselor assists the parents in planning for the immediate and long term needs of the
child including day-to-day care, management, and home training. What are some general goals that the counselor of these
parents should keep in mind?

According to Ehlers, Krishef and Prothero, [4], when parents seek professional help, counseling should be directed
toward:

1. Helping them to be more objective about
   their child.

2. Helping them to learn about behavior their
   child will outgrow and behavior they can
   expect to continue.

3. Helping them to assimilate ideas about handling various problem situations common to
   families of a retarded child.

4. Advising them about the help books and pam-
   phlets can provide and making these materials available for their study and use.

5. Assisting them in learning how to handle
   their retarded child more successfully.

6. Aiding them in helping the child engage in
   leisure-time pursuits and other constructive
   activities which may result in a happier
   child, and therefore, a happier family.

7. Advising them regarding the community resources which are available (e.g., clinics
   education centers, parents' groups, shel-
   tered workshops, and educational institutions for the retarded).

The counselor of parents of the mentally retarded should also remember that parents differ in the quantity and quality of information they can absorb during different phases of the counseling session. Furthermore, there is no single approach in planning for the care and guidance of a retarded child which will be adequate or appropriate to all retarded children. No one approach can be expected to produce the same effect upon the family of every child. An important consideration is that in outlining a program of management and treatment, the family's capacity to follow through on suggestions, in terms of the total family unit, must be kept in mind at all times. As Schild [5] has said, this means that services should be related to the relevant forces of the social structure impinging on the family and which shapes the context in which the family performs its socializing functions. Thus, services, while focused on the needs of the retarded child, should primarily be family-centered and community-concerned. In this regard, The President's Committee on Mental Retardation [6] stressed that:

> "The families of today are subject to many
> stresses and the rate of family breakup is
> alarming. This is, of course, one of the
> conditions in which mental retardation and
> other social ills thrive."

Problems Facing Families

The impact of retardation is felt by all members of the family unit, for mental retardation takes it's toll socially, economically, and emotionally. In general, families of the retarded tend to encounter a greater number of problems in such areas as individual and marital adjustment, child-rearing practices, and sibling relationships. A primary consideration for the counselor is then the problem of mental retardation as it affects human lives, and the development of retarded individuals and of those who live with them. This is, of course, a tremendous undertaking and easier said than done. The responsibility assumed by the counselor is enormous.

Guidelines for the Counselor

Are there guidelines and general directions that the counselor might find helpful in the counseling process? Are there common sense sources of information available to the counselor?

Jordan [7] suggests ten commandments for counselors:

1. Be honest in your appraisal of the situation and explain it without unnecessary delay.

2. Deal with both parents, since they are a natural unit.

3. Be precise, but do not be unnecessarily technical in your explanation.

4. Point out who must be responsible ultimately.

5. Help the parents grasp the issues.

6. Keep in mind the referral agencies that can be of assistance.

7. Avoid precipitating ego-defensive reactions in the parents.

8. Do not expect too much too soon from the parents.

9. Allow parents their quota of concern and uncertainty.

10. Try to crystallize positive attitudes at the onset by using good counseling techniques.

Ehlers, Krishef and Prothero [8] list some principles that should be kept uppermost in mind when counseling parents of a retarded child:

1. First, the counselor should go out of his way if necessary to involve both parents in the counseling process.

2. Give a great deal of support and understanding.

3. Emphasize the value of the feedback interview (question and answer interview) and subsequent follow-up interviews.

4. Urge parents to take advantage of whatever other kind of help and service they may need from community service agencies for the mentally retarded.

5. The counselor should never initiate an interview until he has gathered and understands all
   of the revelant facts concerning the retarded
   child.

6. During the first follow-up interview, the
   counselor should give a prognosis of the
   child's future functioning.

7. The counselor must be sure to base his prognosis on an accurate, carefully conducted
   individual diagnostic evaluation.

8. Agencies should make every effort to preserve
   the continuity of the relationship between
   one main contact person and the parents.

QUESTIONS FOR INDIVIDUAL STUDY AND CLASS DISCUSSION

1. What factors can you cite that can and should relate to
   the decision of institutionalization of the mentally retarded child.

2. How important is it that parents be made aware of the
   varying levels of achievement of retarded children?

3. Why is it important for the counselor to commend any successes parents may have met in the handling of their
   child? What type of counselor-client relationship might
   this help bring about?

4. Is it correct to say that long-range prognosis should at
   all times be presented in a guarded manner, particularly
   in the case of young children?

5. What are some factors you can think of that might be
   directly or indirectly related to the following parental
   reactions? Loss of self-esteem, shame, hostility, demand-
   ingness, rejection, depression, guilt, and self-reproach,
   ambivalence, denial, concern with religion.

6. Discuss the nature, goals, and purposes of genetic counseling. How important is this for parents who may wish
   to have other children?

7. Devise a curriculum for parent education of the families
   with retarded children. What specific subjects (topics)
   would you include? Why?

8. Assuming that the degree of retardation was profound, would you agree or disagree that the most difficult problem for the parents probably centers around the question of whether to place the child in a residential care program or continue to care for him at home.

9. Much research has been done related to "stages" or patterns of behavior that parents go through upon learning they have a retarded child. Review some of these findings and point out any common characteristics. How important is this information for the counselor? How is this related to the counseling process?

10. Discuss the possible causes and ramifications of parents' "shopping behavior," in which they go from one professional to another searching for a ray of hope or even a possible cure.

11. In counseling with parents of the mentally retarded, is it important to avoid saying, "I Understand?" Is it reasonable to assume that unless one has actually experienced the trials and tribulations of these parents, we can only attempt to "understand" on an intellectual level?

12. Discuss the effects, both positive and negative, that the retarded child might have on his siblings. What light does the research shed on this subject?

13. Of the following which <u>one</u> line of approach would be most rewarding in helping parents accept their mentally handicapped child's limitations:

    a. "No one is perfect."

    b. "There is room for everyone in a democracy."

    c. "We all have a contribution to make to society."

    d. "Everyone has his weaknesses."

    e. "If we all work together, he will have a successful life."

14. You are the teacher of a class for the Educable Mentally Retarded. A parent (father) calls the school for an appointment with you because they are very concerned about their child having been placed in your class. From

the tone of the conversation you can tell that they are anxious for "answers." A conference is arranged.

(a) What questions could you anticipate their asking?

(b) How will you explain (or defend) the value of special class placement?

(c) In this situation, what is your role?

(d) They ask about their child's IQ. How do you respond? Can you suggest general guidelines in this area?

REFERENCES

1. Ross, A.O. The Exceptional Child in the Family. New York: Grune & Stratton, 1964, p. 100-101.

2. Stone, M.M. "Parental Attitudes to Retardation," American Journal of Mental Deficiency, 53 (1948), 363.

3. Attwell, A.A. and Clabby, D.A. The Retarded Child: Answers to Questions Parents Ask. Los Angeles: Western Psychological Services, 1971.

4. Ehlers, W.H., Krishef, C.H., and Prothero, J.C. An Introduction to Mental Retardation: A Programmed Text. Columbus, Ohio: Charles E. Merrill, 1973, pp. 185-186.

5. Schild, S. "The Family of the Retarded Child, R.K. Koch and J.C. Dobson (Eds.), The Mentally Retarded Child. New York: Brunner/Mazel, 1971, pp. 431-432.

6. President's Committee on Mental Retardation, National Action to Combat Mental Retardation: A Report to the President. Washington, D.C., 1962, p. 89.

7. Jordan, T.E. The Mentally Retarded. Columbus, Ohio: Charles E. Merrill, 1972, p. 127.

8. Ehlers, Krishef, & Prothero, pp. 189-194.

Chapter 7

COUNSELING PARENTS OF CHILDREN WITH
SPEECH, HEARING, AND VISUAL HANDICAPS

This section on speech, hearing and visual handicaps will not dwell on the technical aspects of these problems. Following a practical definition and brief discussion of each of the disorders, emphasis will be placed upon ways the counselor can assist parents of the handicapped child.

A good parent education program in any area of exceptionality is based in large part on a recognition of individual differences among parents and the provision of activities to meet individual parent needs. According to Carr [1], "the emotional handicap of the parents can be more serious than the handicap of the child, because constructive attitudes and positive action may be too long delayed." The counselor's role is defined by Rittenour [2] when she refers to guidance as the information-giving, recommendation-making functions which help parents define and cope with the facts of their children's problems, and counseling as the process of helping parent's "explore and alleviate their sense of helplessness, anxiousness, and self-condemnation." Beasley [3] further emphasizes the counselor's role as listener: "The (clinician) should listen to what people are saying - really listen - and attempt to understand the emotional impact of the topics parents choose to raise, the problems they describe, the observations they make about their child, and the relationships among family members on which they comment."

Whenever there is a speech or hearing problem there is some degree of breakdown in communication. When parents and child are caught in this vicious circle, this breakdown leads to difficulties in interpersonal relationships which, in turn, lead to further breakdown in communication. In this event, the parent contributes to the child's problems and vice versa. (These communication difficulties often arise during counseling sessions.) Research has shown that counseling can help parents alter the vicious circle of poor communication with their child and establish or reestablish better communication.

According to Webster [4], there are specifically important ways that counseling can provide assistance: First, it can help parents to verbalize frankly about issues in their relationships and forces which motivate them, such as their own needs, goals, and fears. Perhaps this is the most important thing that counseling offers parents: it provides them with a situation in which the clinician is willing for them to be themselves, to disclose their own thoughts and feelings, and to speak of their needs, anxieties, fears, joys, and successes. Second, counseling can provide parents with important information. They need facts, simply and honestly presented about their child's specific disorder. The third way that participation in counseling can help parents is to provide opportunities for them to experiment with tools in the counseling situation and encourage their use. In keeping with the principles of effective counseling, the professional person's role is that of introduction and experimentation with ideas; he cannot make others accept his ideas.

Speech Disorders and Counseling Principles

One of the most widely accepted definitions of a speech disability is the one proposed by Van Riper. According to Van Riper [5], speech may be classified defective under any of three conditions: when it deviates so far from the speech of other people that it draws unfavorable or negative attention to itself, when it interferes with communication, or when speech causes its possessor to be maladjusted. Because of the stress he places on deviation that is "far from the speech of other people," Van Riper's definition implies that we should expect some variability in speech production. When the difference in an individual's speech is viewed as too extreme, then it may be viewed as a disability.

By the same token, one may ask, what is normal speech? Kirk [6] says that "to be normal, speech should permit the undistracted interchange of verbal language, free from grimaces, phonemic misarticulations, unnatural and unusual voice qualities, speaking rates, and rhythms. Vocabulary and sound usage should be adequate and appropriate for the age level, and speech should be delivered in logical, syntactical order."

For practical purposes, five major groups of speech disorders will be briefly discussed. These are as follows: (1) articulation errors such as the use of one sound for another, or the omissions of sounds, such as use of the word "pot" for "spot"; (2) disorders of voice, such as hypernasality and

76

hyponasality, pitch, and volume; (3) stuttering which is characterized by hesitations, repetitions, prolongations, and tension; (4) retarded speech development or delayed speech in which children do not develop the speech expected for their age level, and/or have an inability to use appropriate vocabulary; and (5) speech difficulties due to or associated with cleft palate and/or cleft lip, cerebral palsy, impaired hearing, aphasia and emotional involvement which may manifest itself in speech deviations such as stuttering, and the delay or absence of speech or language. Articulation disorders comprise approximately eighty percent of all speech related problems.

Helping the parents to accept the child with a language disorder is an appropriate first step. The child's speech disorder may stem from a physical, emotional, or cultural source or may be a combination of all these factors. The counselor must aid the parents in recognizing that a problem exists and explain to them that what will be done usually depends on the nature of the problem, its causes, and the child's potential for adjustment.

Parents often desire or welcome information related to procedures for identifying a possible speech disorder of their child. The counselor can be most helpful in this respect by outlining what procedures may be involved in a diagnosis or by stressing the importance of a correct appraisal. There are many ways that evaluations are administered to children. The initial screening of a school-age child may be done by the child's regular teacher using several methods, one being to fill out a "questionnaire - inventory" for each child she finds in her class with a speech deviation which she considers serious enough to warrant further testing or the services of the speech clinician. Another popular way of conducting initial screening is to have the speech clinician visit the classroom and listen and observe children as they recite.

When the teacher concludes, on the basis of her observations, that a child does seem to have a speech problem, a referral should be made to a speech clinician. Certainly, if one is ever in doubt about the existence of a speech or language problem, the speech therapist should be contacted. If the deviation is mild, it may be handled effectively in the classroom with the teacher and clinician jointly working out a program of remediation. In the event the child has a serious handicap, the speech clinician is likely to conduct formal tests.

It should be emphasized that a counselor who has the experience and maturity and is familiar with parental reactions toward handicapping conditions may at this point of diagnosis perform a valuable service to the parents by listening, answering questions within the parents' range of knowledge, and helping them accept and understand the nature of their exceptional child's speech problem and how professional help can be secured. The teacher or counselor should, of course, encourage the parents to seek professional help with difficult or advanced speech disorders. Even a teacher should not undertake formal techniques with advanced stutterers.

Parents should also be assisted in recognizing that the home atmosphere as determined by the personalities of the parents seems to be the most important single factor in influencing the child's acquisition of speech and language. Those aspects of parental behavior which adversely affect the child and his speech must be corrected or modified if he is to make a satisfactory adjustment. Too often, even parents who are greatly concerned about their child's intellectual development make relatively few attempts to assist them in language growth. If there is any evidence of attitudes that are not conducive to good language development, effective counseling is in order. For example, even though professional help is necessary for stutterers, the counselor can offer general information which may be beneficial to the parent in home management. According to Smith [7], it is important to remember that all stutterers will be helped to function more successfully by:

1. Encouraging a great deal of talking in situations likely to bring success - even if this has to begin with choral reading or role playing.

2. Accepting a child's best speech effort without criticism, anxiety, guilt, or anger.

3. Helping the non-fluent child to achieve as much success as possible in non-verbal areas where he is likely to do well.

4. Assisting the non-fluent child in adjusting to his peer group.

5. Avoiding the use of precise labels.

6. Proceeding with caution.

Lundeen [8], even says that "there is evidence that the inci-
dence of stuttering is now less than it was 10 to 15 years
ago. Better parental education about stuttering probably ex-
plains most of the decrement."

Parents may also help their child by assisting the counselor or speech therapist in providing further insights and
information related to the child's speech and language history. If an extensive case history is conducted, the parents
may be asked such questions as:

1. Did speech and language develop at a normal age?

    _____ Yes _____ No Explain _____

2. Are any other languages spoken in the home?

    _____ Yes _____ No If yes, what language? _____

3. Did anyone else in your family have any kind of
   speech therapy?

    _____ Yes _____ No If yes, when, where, and how
                              long?

4. Has your child been evaluated or had any kind of
   speech therapy?

    _____ Yes _____ No If yes, when, where, and how
                              long?

5. When did you first suspect your child might have a
   speech problem?

6. Do you think your child's speech difficulty is:

    _____ Mild _____ Moderate _____ Severe

7. Please give a brief but specific description of
   your child's speech.

One further note on counseling goals. According to Sander [9], the general objectives of the counseling program is reduced to two basic aims:

1. Parents should be supplied with the information they need in order to appreciate the nature of normal childhood speech. They are helped, too, by knowing about the more important conditions under which children - and adults for that matter - are more or less fluent in speech.

2. Parents should be led, so far as possible, to recognize their own insecurities, their excessive psychological need to have their child speak extremely well and perhaps to excel in other ways too, and, in general, their specific discontents and the reasons for them.

It can be readily seen from the foregoing discussion the necessity that parents gain insight into their own attitudes and behavior toward their children. Such understanding appreciably alters and improves the emotional tone of the environment and leads to a closer relationship between parent and child. The most sophisticated and far-reaching program of parent education and/or counseling is of no avail unless parents first come to appropriate and realistic feelings, not only toward and about their exceptional child but also about conflicts and confusion which may exist within themselves.

Hearing Impairments and Counseling Principles

As we have observed in the previous section on speech handicaps, parents may need help in accepting their roles, and in modifying their feelings of guilt and anxiety. As Barsch, [10] has so aptly put it:

No parent is ever prepared to be the parent of a handicapped child. It is a post hoc identity which is learned in the day-by-day laboratory of the home-school-clinic-triad. It is this learning which must occupy our attention. Each professional must become fully cognizant of the parent as a learner with the content area of learning being the special child. The humanity of the parent identifies him as a special learner - his parenthood of a special child represents a particular emphasis in learning. It is the parent's efficiency as a learner which is critical to the point we are trying to make.

We must therefore, capitalize on the parent as a learner. Karnes and Zehrbach [11] say that the success of a parental involvement program is contingent upon:

1. The attitude of the professional - there must be a positive attitude which connotes that parents have a contribution to make to the growth of their child.

2. Recognition that there is more than one way to involve parents - parents have individual needs that must be recognized to help them select the best way to involve themselves in the educational program of their child at a given time.

3. The belief that each parent is capable of growth - the amount of growth of parents will vary. The extent to which a parent progresses is dependent upon the degree to which the teacher changes, expands, and increases the breadth and depth of activities in the parent involvement program.

Love [12] suggests the following as constructive ways of meeting the needs of parents of deaf children:

Even after parents have made a realistic adjustment to their child's problem and have accepted him as a deaf or hard-of-hearing child and have made the best arrangements possible in their situation for his education and future; even then they need help in understanding and accepting their feelings and attitudes toward him.

Parents of deaf children, in particular, need help in avoiding the strains of being overly conscientious and self-conscious about their responsibilities as parents. Like many parents today, they need encouragement to relax and enjoy their children. Therefore, all parents at times need help in maintaining a healthy attitude of realistic acceptance and understanding of the situation.

The counselor can play another important role in assisting these parents by stressing the importance of a correct diagnosis. As stated by Hedgecock [13]:

> An accurate and authoritative evaluation of the hearing problem of a child suspected of having hearing disability is an important first step in bringing the parents to grips with the problem. It is the only hope available for ending the frequently futile search for a diagnosis of normalcy and preoccupation with unrealistic hopes for curative treatment.
>
> Contrary to some belief it surely is an ultimate kindness to parents to be told as early and as accurately as possible the condition of their child's hearing. Certainly it is the only approach that does justice to the child. Acceptance of the situation must be followed by understanding of the problem and of the procedures to be employed in alleviating or compensating for the condition. The discovery or the confirmation that their child has a hearing impairment frequently causes an emotional reaction on the part of the parents which must be resolved to some extent before intelligent understanding and management is possible.

It is not uncommon for parents of a deaf child to want to know what to do to promote development of the speech and language of their child and how to communicate with their deaf child. One parent [14] refers specifically to this when she writes of her experience with her son:

> It is urgent that parents be referred immediately to someone who can teach them how to communicate with their deaf child orally and manually, yet it is rarely done.
>
> Because deafness is an invisible disability, the average person has no understanding of its implications. Being born deaf or losing one's hearing before language has developed imposes a critical barrier to a deaf child's ability to learn about the world in which he must live. Ignoring deafness does not make it go away and unless adequate and meaningful methods of communication are developed with siblings and parents, emotional problems will almost surely develop among members of the family.

This section will conclude with another meaningful way in which the counselor can suggest for proper home management of the deaf or hard-of-hearing child. Parents often overcompensate for deafness by shielding their son or daughter from competition with hearing children. As Love [15] notes, "When parents discover that they have a deaf child, they must accept the fact that the child is to be treated as much like a normal child as possible. Perhaps the only good thing about the parents not discovering their child's deafness at an early age is that they treat him as normal when they think that he is normal. The more normally the child is treated, the better adjusted he and his family will be." Heisler [16] also makes this observation, "Except for the child's basic security-need, which is fulfilled through parental love, there is no psychological need more important to the child's later maturity and stability than the development of his potential for self-direction. This fact has not been understood by thousands of parents who have tried to apply the psychologically popular concept of permissiveness and have thereby released their children to a state of freedom from discipline without accompanying nurturance of the child's inner resources for responsible and productive functioning."

Counseling with Parents of the Visually Handicapped

According to Harley [17] children with visual disabilities are those who differ from the average to such a degree that special personnel, curriculum, adaption, and/or additional instructional materials are needed to assist them in achieving at a level commensurate with their abilities. The terms "visual impairment," "vision loss," or "vision problem" refer to the physical loss of part of all of useful vision.

A more technical definition is offered in The National Society for the Prevention of Blindness Fact Book [18]:

Blindness is generally defined in the United States as visual acuity for distance vision 20/20 or less in the better eye, with best correction; or visual acuity of more than 20/200 if the widest diameter of field of vision subtends an angle no greater than 20 degrees.

83

The partially seeing are defined as persons with
a visual acuity greater than 20/200 but not
greater than 20/70 in the better eye with correction.

The role of the counselor in counseling parents of the
visually impaired is described by Warnick [19] as follows:
"The good counselor listens; shares information; is well-in-
formed about available services and referral procedure; does
not make decisions for the family but lets the family work
through their own feelings to a possible solution. He sees
the parent as a parent and not primarily as a patient. Furthermore, he has worked through his deep-seated attitudes, toward various handicaps. He, of course, has had training and
experience."

While focus is often centered on the blind child, the parents also often encounter emotional and psychological problems. As Van den Broek [20] has described it,

It is natural, in fact almost inevitable, that
when parents discover they have a blind baby
they are not only sorrowed but shocked . . . .
Almost all young parents who find their child is
blind are shocked and confused . . . . It is
the tendency of most of us faced with misfortune
to rebel, and to wonder why it had to happen to
us.

These parental reactions may run the gamut from shock and
grief to bewilderment and helplessness. Parents may need help
in the analysis of their needs too, for when they are upset
and confused, their effect upon the child will be counterpro-
ductive to his maximum adjustment and development. Love [21],
in speaking of parental attitudes, makes this comment:

Parents are the most important persons in the
social environment of the child and their attitudes profoundly affect his life. Parents must
discover that the essential needs of their blind
or partially sighted child are the same as those
of children with normal vision. The parents
must learn to think in terms of what he is and
what he has rather than in terms of what he lacks.
They must learn to make the child happy with
himself by dwelling on what he can do, and not
his handicap. It takes a mentally mature family
to meet this challenge. If the family accepts
the child, others will also.

Parents also need help in terms of information and long-range planning. The problems and frustrations which the parents may have with the home management procedure and routine can be overwhelming. Areas such as mobility, language development, personal and social adjustment and perceptual and conceptual processes are, of course, significant, in the child's progress and development. Home chores such as eating, dressing, and playing, present a bewildering array of frustrating, and heartrending problems and difficulties. Given guidance, direction and support, parents however, need not remain in a state of hopelessness, despair, and confusion.

The counselor must be knowledgeable in assisting the parents in home management. This is illustrated by Telford and Sawrey [22] when they write:

> The visually impaired child is much more dependent on auditory, principally verbal, sources for his motivation. The many bumps and bruises he will get arouse the anxiety of those about him because of the real as well as the exaggerated danger he invites. This and the over-protection afforded him add to his inherent disability and increase his handicap. Although independent locomotion - the ability to move about freely and independently at home, in the neighborhood, and in traffic - is of primary importance to the blind, it has only recently begun to receive the attention it warrants. It is obvious that these skills, which the sighted individual learns largely incidentally and with little formal instruction, must become a matter of primary concern in the training of the blind.

> Such training begins in the home, where situations must be deliberately contrived to encourage the blind child - to become curious and explore his world. The blind child needs a wealth of sounds, objects within reach, and even odors which he is encouraged to find and explore.

In fact, it is unlikely that supportive and reassuring counseling is sufficient if practical help in home management and daily care of the child is not also available. For the parent to actually see the child progress in some of the basic home skills as, for example, toilet training, mobility, and feeding may do more to mold favorable attitudes than hours of dialogue between the counselor and parents. Parents will be more accepting of their partially sighted or blind child if the child shows physical and mental development, if he is responsive and is learning to make progress even with relatively simple tasks. In order to accomplish this, parents need intensive individual counseling and/or supportive services from other disciplines such as medicine, social work, and psychology. A multidisciplinary team can provide services to the parents and children who could not be cared for by any single member of that team working independently.

This chapter will close with a quote from Cerulli and Shugerman [23],

> In conclusion, we feel that the blind child should be treated as a normal person with the awareness of the handicap, so that special provisions can be made to permit normal maturational development. We feel that no progress can be achieved, either in early infancy or in the age group of our children, unless the parents are given specific concrete suggestions with respect to helping their children learn about their environment. In the last analysis, it is the parents who have the most influence in the child's life. Without the foregoing, he will vegetate.

QUESTIONS FOR INDIVIDUAL STUDY OR CLASS DISCUSSION

1. To understand speech disorders, why is it necessary to know certain facts about normal speech including its development and production?

2. How can one attempt to explain why defective speech tends to demoralize its possessor and often causes reactions such as guilt, resentment, hostility, withdrawal, and/or aggression? Why can the answer to this question be significant to both the counselor and parents?

3. Would you defend or refute the viewpoint that holds that the cultural milieu in which children are growing up in present-day America places increasing emphasis on the vital importance of all forms of communication: listening, speaking, reading, and writing? What evidence can you cite or suggest?

4. Give some specific examples or undertake as a research project, a study of the home backgrounds of children in an effort to explain why some develop language and speech disorders and others do not?

5. In general, are parents likely to come to the speech clinician with any degree of insight about their child's speech deviation? In terms of insight, what factors do you consider important? Why?

6. Should the counseling session for the parents of a speech handicapped child be structured?

7. The following is a list of frequently used terms associated with auditory impairments. Can you define these terms? Could you explain their meaning to parents without using sophisticated technical jargon?

   decibels, otologist, speechreading, auditory training, oralism, manualism, fingerspelling, the simultaneous approach, audiometer, residual hearing, Rochester method,

8. Parents with whom you are counseling express concern about their visually impaired child's personal and social adjustment. What does the research tell us that we can share with these parents?

9. Are there agencies, diagnostic clinics, or other facilities in your community, county, city, or state that offer comprehensive professional services which should serve to strengthen the relationship between parents and the visually handicapped child and give parents the information and skills that would enable them to meet the child's special needs?

10. How would you explain to the parents the difference between residential schools, day school, and special classes for deaf children? What are the advantages and disadvantages?

11. Why is it important for parents and relatives to realize that the child has limitations as well as potentials? In the counseling process, should the counselor emphasize the child's limitations or potentials or give both approximately equal consideration?

12. To what extent do you think that parents intellectually understand the problems of the handicapped child? By way of contrast, to what extent do they accept the child's handicap on an emotional level? What factors may account for this?

13. Unless we have had the personal experiences of rearing a speech, hearing, or visually handicapped child, it is almost impossible to emphathize with the parents. In light of this statement, what is the counselor's role?

14. For an advanced research topic, trace the history of parent counseling.

15. In the past, etiology, diagnosis, and parental attitudes have been the most emphasized aspects of parental counseling. How can counseling not only be based just on today's services but also with services likely to be developed in the future?

16. Debate: Teachers in training need as much preparation in working with parents and other professional personnel as they do in working with children.

REFERENCES

1. Carr, L.B. "Problems Confronting Parents of Children with Handicaps," Exceptional Child, 25 (1959), 253.

2. Rittenour, M. "Counseling with Parents of Children with Abnormal Speech and Language Development," Jr. Med. Assoc. of Alabama, 34 (1964), 62-65.

3. Beasley, J. "Relationship of Parental Attitudes to Development of Speech Problems," Journal of Speech and Hearing Disorders, 21 (1956), 317-321.

4. Webster, E.J. "Parent Counseling by Speech Pathologists and Audiologists," Journal of Speech and Hearing Disorders, 31 (1966), 317-321.

5. Van Riper, C. Speech Correction: Principles and Methods. 5th Edition. Englewood Cliffs, N.J.: Prentice-Hall, 1972.

6. Kirk, S.A. Educating Exceptional Children. 2nd Ed.
   Boston,: Houghton Mifflin, 1972, p. 74.

7. Smith, R.M. Teacher Diagnosis of Educational Difficulties.
   Columbus, Ohio: Charles E. Merrill, 1969, pp. 135-136.

8. Lundeen, D.J. "Speech Disorders." In B.R. Gearheart (Ed.),
   Education of the Exceptional Child. Scranton, Penn.:
   Intext Educational Publishers, 1972. p. 159.

9. Sander, E.K. "Counseling Parents of Stuttering Children,"
   Journal of Speech and Hearing Disorders, 24 (1959),
   262-271.

10. Barsch, R.H. The Parent Teacher Partnership. The Council
    for Exceptional Children, Inc. 1969, pp. 49-50.

11. Karnes, M.B. & Zehrback, R.R. "Flexibility in Getting Pa-
    rents Involved in the School," Teaching Exceptional
    Children, (Fall, 1972), 7.

12. Love, H.D. Parental Attitudes Toward Exceptional Children.
    Springfield, Ill.: Charles C. Thomas, 1970, p. 128.

13. Hedgecock, L.D. "Counseling the Parents of Acoustically
    Handicapped Children." In R.L. Noland (Ed.),
    Counseling Parents of the Ill and the Handicapped.
    Springfield, Ill.: Charles C. Thomas, 1971, pp. 369-370.

14. Rhodes, M.J. "Invisible Barrier," The Exceptional Parent,
    (April/May, 1972), p. 13.

15. Love, p. 129.

16. Heisler, V. A Handicapped Child in the Family: A Guide
    for Parents. New York: Grune & Stratton, 1972,
    pp. 103-104.

17. Harley, R.K. "Children with Visual Disabilities." In
    Dunn, L.M. (Ed.), Exceptional Children in the Schools.
    New York: Holt, Rinehart and Winston, 1973, p. 413.

18. National Society for the Prevention of Blindness. N.S.P.B.
    Fact Book: Estimated Statistics on Blindness and
    Visual Problems. New York, 1966, p. 10.

19. Warnick, L. "The Effect Upon a Family of a Child with a Handicap," The New Outlook for the Blind, (December, 1969)

20. Van den Broek, G. Guide for Parents of a Preschool Blind Child. New York State Department of Social Work, New York, 1945, p. 13.

21. Love, p. 137.

22. Telford, C.W. & Sawrey, J.M. The Exceptional Individual. Englewood Cliffs, New Jersey: Prentice Hall, 1972, p. 309.

23. Cerulli, F. & Shugerman, E.E. "Infancy: Counseling the Family," New Outlook for the Blind, 55 (1961), 297.

Chapter 8

COUNSELING PARENTS OF THE PHYSICALLY HANDICAPPED CHILD

Physical handicaps as used in this chapter refer to a wide range of disabilities including neurological, muscular, skeletal, and general physical difficulties. The physically handicapped child may have a major disability such as cerebral palsy, muscular dystrophy, or spina bifida or an infectious disease such as hepatitis, nephritis and mononucleosis.

Parental Attitudes

As Love [1] has stated, the impact of the physically handicapped child on the family unit educes many different attitudinal patterns. These attitudes may be newly formed or merely intensified examples of those parental emotions classified as "first reactions." In addition, each parent will bring to the situation his own unique perceptions of the child and the handicap, and his own assets and limitations for handling his role in the situation.

Parents' poor attitudes have often proved a stumbling block to the successful treatment-training program of youngsters who have physical handicaps. For example, rejection of the child with a physical handicap appears to be very common among parents. When parents have inadequate coping skills and cannot adapt in a positive manner toward their child they often exhibit an attitude of indifference, or rejection.

Parental rejection is difficult to determine because it is usually an observed diagnosis by others rather than an admission by the parents. As noted by Hutt and Gibby [2], "because, the parent is not aware of the basis of his own feelings toward him, and consequently he experiences severe conflicts."

Other common initial reactions which are frequently experienced by parents of a physically handicapped child include (1) anxiety, (2) grief, (3) disbelief, (4) ambivalence, (5) emotional distress, (6) shock, (7) anger, and (8) disappointment. It should be pointed out that in spite of these negative and adverse reactions, some family reactions to a physical disability are excellent. As Jordan [3] has observed, "Excellence in this content has several connotations. An excellent reaction may be no reactions; when disability is mild, a family may find its routines altered only slightly and its expectations barely modified. Excellence may be attributed to realistic and therapeutically oriented attitudes toward a child with serious limitations." In discussing the ecology of disability Jordan closes with this note, "unfortunately, bad attitudes are usually more difficult to eradicate and feelings of guilt and worry may be suppressed, only to appear as irritation and petulance among members of the family."

Inappropriate feelings of guilt, anxiety and emotional distress probably occur with greater frequency among parents of the physically handicapped. One author [4] has observed that most parents of children with severe diseases such as leukemia, cystic fibrosis, cerebral palsy, and brain injury exhibit at one time or another an inappropriate guilt reaction concerning their child's illness. The counselor often hears such comments as these:

> "It's my fault he got measles encephalitis.
> I shouldn't have sent him to camp."

> "We had sexual relations during the last
> month of pregnancy. Maybe that did it."

> "God punished me for not going to church."

One of the major causes of guilt feelings is the lack of information concerning the child's handicapping condition and the causes of it. Regardless of whether the guilt is due to unconscious hostility, lack of accurate information, or other mechanisms, it is best resolved through its understanding and analysis.

Principles of Counseling

This section will identify some general principles and procedures, that are usually appropriate in counseling parents of a physically handicapped child. The nature and degree of the child's physical disability, the personality of the handicapped child, the understanding and coping skills of the parents, and the skill and knowledge of the counselor constitute some of the important variables which ultimately influence the scope, nature and direction of the counseling process. Depending, then, on a careful analysis of each individual situation, the counselor may find many of the following principles to be valuable.

The counselor should stress to the parents that physically handicapped children have the same needs as all children, as well as some that are uniquely their own. In a very real sense, the physically handicapped child is not different from the normal. While many parents of the handicapped child may adopt a defeatist attitude, the counselor is a supportive person who can focus their attention to the hopeful facts - the child's strengths and his potential for improvement. This concept is closely tied to assisting the parent with the acceptance of their child. As Robinson and Robinson [5] have stated "acceptance of the retarded child, as of the normal child, involved warm appreciation of his individuality, pride in his assets, and tolerance for his shortcoming." Is there reason to believe that this does not hold true for the physically handicapped as well?

The counselor, therefore, must be a person capable of effecting attitudinal change. Love [6] contends that "parental counseling involves many therapeutic and diagnostic processes. In counseling parents of the physically handicapped child these processes are directed toward a goal of acceptance, adapting present behavior and understanding parental reaction."

The counselor must also be a person who can emphasize the parent-child relationship. As Mosher and Stewart [7] said, "One of the most important factors to keep in mind in parent counseling is the quality of parent-child relationships." Problems which may be encountered due to physical handicaps are either reinforced or reduced according to the impact of the family members on the person. "Family therapy" continues to be a trend and is enjoying increasing popularity in child guidance clinics, hospitals, and other treatment facilities.

Another counselor role is assisting parents to a full realization that the physically handicapped - in spite of possible disabilities - should not expect to receive their sympathy. Children, like adults, sense a deep need to be understood and fully accepted in the social world. While the disability may be mild, moderate, or severe, the parents should never attempt to do everything for the child. The degree of physical handicap will determine to a great extent how much the parents should attempt to do for the child. As home "behavior modifiers," the parents must constantly instill in the child the desire to achieve. Because of the impact of the home environment, everything that parents do will directly or indirectly affect the personalities of their offspring. Also, the dynamics of the behavior and personality that go to make up the child will often determine the attitudes of the parents. This is to suggest that children develop problems of their own and this is often complicated because the disabled child has still other influences impinging upon him.

Because the physically handicapped child so often experiences difficulties in making direct contact with their environment, the counselor should assist the parents (as well as the school) so that their environment is adapted to their special needs whenever possible. The physically handicapped child has to perceive his world in many ways before he can understand and eventually begin to master aspects of it. Given the know-how and encouragement, parents can utilize self-instruction efficiently, informing themselves about their responsibilities. Furthermore, parents should be encouraged to investigate the literature pertaining to physical handicaps, to contact other professionals, and to actively seek out parents with similar problems and concerns.

In many instances, the education of physical handicapped children has to be based on the combined efforts of many people: teachers, physicians, psychologists, therapists, social workers, paraprofessionals and, most importantly, their parents. The counselor has a responsibility to his clients not only to be knowledgeable about the availability of such services when needed and when a referral should be made. In this regard, moral support is especially significant for the insecure parent and the offer of concrete services together with the recognition that their task will not be an easy one may be considered a counselor responsibility.

Being the parents of a physically handicapped child can often put a financial burden on the family. The knowledgeable, resourceful counselor can and should recognize such a problem and help to find some relief for the parents. As Gearheart [8] has so aptly commented, "In our society, the disabled child should not suffer from lack of care because the family finances cannot entirely provide the payments."

In conclusion, the words of Reid [9] seem very appropriate, "To care for a crippled child under a heavy burden of guilt is a heavy task. The guilt-laden parent needs help immediately. He needs counseling, education, services - everything that will help him regard the handicapped child not as a punishment but as an accident. When his energies are no longer totally inverted in inner conflict but free to make plans and find care for the child, then the whole family including the handicapped child, stand to gain immeasurable." As members of the helping profession can we effectively assist parents in this endeavor? If our answer is not a resounding "yes," then should we leave this important task to others? The reader must make a value judgment in this regard. For the sake of the parent and child we cannot afford the luxury of using poor judgment.

QUESTIONS FOR INDIVIDUAL STUDY AND CLASS DISCUSSION

1. Interview children and youth who have physical handicaps. What type of challenges and frustrations did they (or do they still) face?

2. Interview parents of children with physical handicaps. Identify past and future concerns that they have about their child. What unique problems do parents of the physically handicapped face when compared with other handicapping conditions?

3. Discuss the viewpoint that a physical disability is not an objective thing in a person, but a social value judgment. Does society label a disability by creating a culture in which certain tools are required for behavior?

4. Because of special needs like transportation, prosthetic and orthotic devices, and prescriptions for medicine necessary for the adequate health and well-being for the child, the parents are often faced with financial distress. Identify and outline the services and/or financial assistance available fron national, state, and local agencies and organizations. Include such groups as the State Public Health or Welfare Department, United Cerebral Palsy Association, Muscular Dystrophy Association, and the Cystic Fibrosis Association.

5. Are there civic clubs or organizations in your community which might assist parents of physically handicapped children?

6. You are counseling with the parent of a physically handicapped child. The parent says, "But I have my own life
   to lead." What implication may be drawn from this statement. Remembering the effective counseling techniques
   discussed earlier in this text, how would (could) you respond to such a statement. List and discuss some appropriate responses. List and discuss some inappropriate responses. What other factors need to be considered or information gathered to respond intelligently?

7. What types of public and private school services are available in your community for the physically handicapped?

8. Assuming that the information at your disposal suggests
   that placement in a special class facility is warranted
   and that the parents either reject or question such placement for their child, what response do you make? What
   recources are available to the parent?

9. Discuss the role that physical, occupational, and speech
   therapy may play in the education and treatment of a
   physically handicapped child. Explain the nature and purposes of these services?

10. Discuss nutrition and the total process of feeding child-
    ren with motor disabilities. Is this an important con-
    sideration? If so, why?

11. Visit a local special class (or facility) for the physi-
    cally handicapped. What observations did you make to broad-
    en your understanding about the problems of the physi-
    cally handicapped. As an alternative, ask a certified
    teacher of the physically handicapped to visit your
    class and discuss his work both with the handicapped and
    with parents.

12. Invite a staff member from an organization such as the
    United Cerebral Palsy Association to visit your class and
    discuss their work with children who have physical handi-
    caps. How extensive is their work in counseling with
    the parents? Do they have a parent-training program?

REFERENCES

1. Love, H.D. Parental Attitudes Toward Exceptional Children.
   Springfield, Ill: Charles C. Thomas, 1970, p. 80.

2. Hutt, M.L. & Gibby, R.G. The Mentally Retarded Child:
   Development, Education and Treatment. 2nd Edition
   Boston: Allyn and Bacon, 1965, p. 311.

3. Jordan, T.E. "Physical Disability in Children and Family
   Adjustment." Rehabilitation Literature Vol. 24.
   1963, pp. 330-336.

4. Gardner, R.A. "The Guilt Reaction of Parents of Children
   with Severe Physical Disease," American Journal of
   Psychiatry, 26 (1969), 636-644.

5. Robinson, H.B. & Robinson, N.M. The Mentally Retarded
   Child: A Psychological Approach. New York: McGraw-
   Hill, 1965, p. 512.

6. Love, p. 82.

7. Mosher, F.S. & Stewart, M. "Parents Expectations in Planning for Their Child's Rehabilitation," Exceptional
   Children, 25 (1958), 120.

8. Gearheart, B.R. Education of the Exceptional Child.
   Scranton, Penn." Intext Educational Publishers,
   1972, p. 246.

9. Reid, E.S. "Helping Parents of Handicapped Children,"
   Children, Vol. 5 (1968), p. 19.

Chapter 9

COUNSELING PARENTS OF CHILDREN WITH
SPECIFIC LEARNING DISABILITIES

As a descriptive term or category, "learning disabilities" is relatively new to the field of special education. As Gearheart [1] says, "If a field is an entity only as long as it has been generally recognized as a total related area, 'learning disabilities' is very new. An example of this newness would be the fact that the first journal with national distribution, including the term 'learning disabilities' in its title, was the Journal of Learning Disabilities, which was first published in January, 1968."

It was not until the early 1960's that the term "learning disabilities" began to appear with any frequency and then it was used mainly as a substitute for "minimally brain-injured." National legislative recognition for learning disabilities as an educational category came when "The Children with Learning Disabilities Act of 1969" passed the House of Representatives by a roll call of 350 to zero. Even as we move into the mid 1970's, the field of learning disabilities is still enjoying popularity and growing at a phenomenally rapid rate.

Definitions

There are a number of definitions of learning disabilities. Kirk [2] has proposed that: "A learning disability refers to a specific retardation or disorder in one or more of the processes of speech, language, perception, behavior, reading, spelling, writing, or arithmetic."

Because of national interest in the problem and both state and federal legislation, the National Advisory Committee on Handicapped Children of the U.S. Office of Education [3] used the following definition in the Congressional bill entitled "The Learning Disabilities Act of 1969":

> Children with special (specific) learning disabilities exhibit a disorder in one or more of the basic psychological processes involved in understanding or in using spoken or written language. These may be

manifested in disorders of listening, thinking, talking, reading, writing, spelling, or arithmetic. They include conditions which have been referred to as perceptual handicaps, brain injury, minimal brain dysfunction, dyslexia, developmental aphasia, etc. They do not include learning problems which are due primarily to visual, hearing, or motor handicaps, to mental retardation, emotional disturbance, or to environmental disadvantage.

McCarthy and McCarthy [4] refer to an earlier study by Clements in which he analyzed almost a hundred behavioral characteristics of the child with learning disabilities. The ten most frequently cited characteristics of such children are:

1. Hyperactivity

2. Perceptual-motor deficits

3. Emotional liability

4. General orientation defects

5. Disorders of attention such as distractibility and short attention span

6. Impulsivity

7. Disorders of memory and conceptual thinking

8. Specific learning disabilities in reading, arithmetic, writing, and spelling

9. Disorders of speech and hearing

10. Equivocal neurological signs and electroncephalographic irregularities

Telford and Sawrey [5] offer a practical viewpoint of learning disabilities which emphasizes educational intervention. They say:

The term "learning disabilities" implies diagnosis that is primarily educational and remediation that is teacher-learner oriented. The term also suggests a program of positive action and appropriate teaching. It does not suggest an inherent and largely static condition as the term "mental retardation" does. The name contains a plea for good teaching based on the child's specific needs.

The term is relatively nonstigmatizing and designates a specific deficit in children who are essentially normal and focuses attention on identifying the child's specific needs and applying appropriate remedial procedure rather than becoming excessively concerned with etiology and proper labelling.

Diagnosis of Learning Disabilities

It is in the area of diagnosis that the counselor can offer constructive information to concerned parents. Because "learning disabilities" covers such a wide array of disorders, the parent will likely be concerned about the exact nature of their child's disorder and the prospects for remediation. A counselor should have basic knowledge of the diagnostic procedure and should be able to convey these findings to the parents in a concise, straightforward manner.

Children with learning disabilities are a heterogeneous group, and the type and degree of learning disorder varies widely from one person to another. The diagnostic process is, therefore, a critical first-step in determining the approaches and techniques that will be used as guidelines for effective educational intervention. Lerner [6] lists the following as essential in making the diagnosis:

1. Determine whether the child has a learning disability.

2. Measure the child's present achievement to detect in what specific area he is failing and at what levels he appears to be blocked.

3. Analyze how the child learns.

4. Explore why he is not learning.

5. Collate and interpret data and formulate a diagnostic hypothesis.

6. Develop a plan for teaching in the light of the hypothesis that has been formulated.

The counselor is well-advised to stress to the parents the importance of securing a comprehensive diagnosis that will yield the most accurate analysis of the child's disorder. Unless the counselor has had formal training in learning disabilities, or has certain competencies, it is advisable to leave the diagnosis to a trained person. Competencies include a broad background in child development, learning theory, and basic teaching skills; understanding of learning problems including characteristics of a typical learning pattern and casual factors contributing to learning failure; and skills in assessment and selection, administration, and scoring of standardized tests.

Parents can often play a vital role in the collection of data for their child's diagnosis. A case history is normally a part of the diagnostic procedure and is important because it provides both general information and insights related to the child's background and development. The following kinds of information may be obtained from the parents: the child's prenatal history, birth conditions, and neonatal development; the child's health and medical history, and personal, social, and family history. As emphasized in Part I of this text, a skilled interviewer who establishes feelings of mutual trust and understanding can obtain a maximum amount of useful data from parents. Lerner [7] specifically speaks to this by stating:

> He (the interviewer) must be careful not to alarm parents by his questions nor to make them defensive because they suspect his disapproval of their actions. His attitude should convey a spirit of cooperation and acceptance. Though he should show empathy for problems, he must maintain a degree of professional objectivity.

> If the history taking is to be useful in making a diagnosis, it must go beyond routine questions and gather more information and impressions than the questions themselves ask. The skillful interviewer is able to gather information in a smooth, conversation-like manner while fulfilling all the other requirements of case study techniques.

The Need for a Different Approach

Working effectively with parents of children with learning disabilities may suggest a somewhat different approach for the educator, especially when compared with other handicapping disorders. As Barsch [8] critically comments:

> Educators must become fully cognizant that the parent of the child with a learning disability represents a somewhat different challenge to the world of special education than has been the case with parents in the past. The child with a learning disability is not a unitary composite of a fixed set of characteristics (a great deal of disagreement exists among professionals regarding an acceptable wording of a definition for this child.) If the professional world of education lacks clarity of definition, if teacher qualifications for serving this child are vague or nonexistent, if collegiate preparation programs are only now beginning to emerge and develop to serve this need, then there can be no doubt that the parents of these children are also bewildered.

McCarthy and McCarthy [9] also suggest the need for a different approach or outlook when they make the following observation:

> The parents of children with learning disabilities suffer a frustration not usually associated with the more dramatic handicaps. For want of a better phrase, we call it the "taste of honey" phenomenon. In many of the emotionally disturbed, and in all of the children with learning disabilities, intelligence is essentially normal. The contrast of the normal and subnormal abilities within each of these children seems to create a constant irritation for the parent because in many ways the child does behave normally, which only makes one long all the more for that educational, medical, or psychiatric treatment which can push the child to complete normalcy. Having tasted the "honey" of normalcy in their children, they understandably yearn for more. This inevitably leads to a certain amount of frustration, which is not experienced by parents

of children with more devastating handicaps who are not offered this promise.

In view of the comments by Barsch and McCarthy and
McCarthy, the implications are clear - we need to distinguish
the unique character of learning disabilities and to clearly
differentiate this child from other special education children.
We need to develop a proper prospective for the field of learning disabilities. Finally, we must learn to assist parents so
that they will be adequately equipped to deal with the problems
of their child with learning disabilities.

Counseling with Parents - Issues and Procedures

When counseling with parents of a child with a learning
disorder, the counselor should consciously strive to avoid the
use of technical, clinical terminology. Terms such as dysfunction, perseveration, syndrome, apraxia, disgraphia, later-
ality, impulsivity, modality, and perceptual disorders should
be tools of the trade and rarely should be used by the counselor in the interview or conference with parents. Ellingson
[10] illustrates this point in her book, The Shadow Children
when she says:

> The most important single factor that is
> common to the plight of all these children
> is ignorance, but it is not the ignorance
> of indifference. Most parents love their
> children, most want to help them - if they
> can. But, they need information - to give
> them clues to the nature of their child's
> problems, and a plan of action for amelior-
> ating it. Too often the professionals
> have walled layman off from the necessary
> knowledge through the use of clinical lan-
> guage.

Another important principle of counseling is to help the
parents understand they they must not shoulder the entire blame
for their child's learning disorder. As Brown [11] has commented:

> Society usually assumes that behavior is
> the result of upbringing. When a child
> fails to meet society's expectations, he
> is blamed and so are the parents. Often,
> parents are their own harshest critics,
> taking all the blame for the impulsive,

disruptive, aggressive, or anti-social
acts of children with neurological impairment of attention, learning, or
impulse. Parents can try to provide
opportunities, good examples, and good
training, but they cannot take blame
when things do not go right all of the
time.

Brown summarizes his suggestions for parents by saying
that, "When a child and his family need help with controls,
behavior, or learning, many things can be done. The key pro-
visions seem to be: (1) understanding the individual child's
disability, (2) providing loving firmness, (3) structuring
the environment, (4) setting good examples and high standards,
and (5) providing opportunities to succeed, to build self-
esteem and to feel wanted."

It is also important that counseling parents of children
with learning disorders begins as soon as possible. Early intervention is, without question, preferable to action taken
after a parent is concerned because the disorder may be complicated or worsen because of "too little, too late." Bryant
[12] states that early counseling may assist parents in understanding the following:

(1) They have a responsibility to their children, not to
    themselves, and that if the rehabilitation programs
    are to be at all successful, they must allow their
    children the emotional freedom to profit from the
    program.

(2) They must realize that the program is not designed
    to prove that they are worthy parents, but rather to
    help their children in their adjustment to society.

(3) They must maintain a consistent and accepting atti-
    tude and not become discouraged or overzealous by
    slow or rapid progress.

Parents often encounter difficulties in implementing home
programs for children with learning disabilities. Neifert and
Gayton [13] address themselves to this problem and reasons for
the frequent failures. As the authors suggest, a discussion
of these family types will allow professional personnel to
make better decisions regarding utilization of home programs.

Several "high risk" family types are identified in this study by Neifert and Gayton. The first group consists of families in which the mother feels that something is wrong with the child but receives little or no support for her views from the father. A second type of family in which home programs fail is the family in which a power struggle exists between mother and child. A third type of family which often experiences difficulties with a home program is the multiple-program family. This type of family has so many other problems that the potential for success of a home program is questionable from the start. Parents faced with serious marital, financial, and/or health problems find it extremely difficult to allocate the time necessary for a regular home program. The fourth type of family that has difficulty with a home program is the family with a large number of children. The authors found that the mother usually cannot find time to monitor a home program because of the realistic demands made on her to carry out the normal functions of everyday family life.

In conclusion, the authors note that the ideal circumstances for utilization of a home program are to some extent the opposite of the four family types described. They note, too, the necessity of looking at the total family process and actively oppose attempts on the part of clinicians to use the home program solely as a means of fulfilling their obligation to the family.

As teachers, counselors, or other types of professionals, we must actively seek practical ways to involve parents in their childrens' developmental lags. The parent who has sought counseling and accepted her child's learning disability is prone to be an effective team member. This parent will be conscientious in keeping appointments, will seek and utilize direction and advice regarding her child's disability, and will follow through on suggested home management programs. This point is further illustrated in an article by DeGenaro [14] entitled "What Do You Say When A Parent Asks, How Can I Help My Child?" In this article she describes practical techniques for strengthening the child's visual modality with minimal cost and without special equipment.

This section has attempted to identify a few of the principles that the skilled counselor should be knowledgeable about when working with parents of children with learning disabilities. The author will conclude this chapter by sharing with the reader the following editorial comment [15]:

> ....a parent who understands his child's abili-
> ties and disabilities can help the child to un-
> derstand himself in order to function better in
> whatever conditions life imposes on him. A pa-
> rent who is "on top" of a complex situation can
> do a lot to support his child when he is called
> "stupid" or "dumb" simply because he is not run-
> ning as fast either physically, intellectually,
> or emotionally as the others. A parent who is
> uninformed and bewildered by it all is unlikely
> to keep his own perspective where it should be,
> and certainly will be unable to help his child
> to recognize when the problem lies not in him-
> self, but in others. We are all a long way
> from appreciating individual differences. Teach-
> ers, parents, and peers often make life doubly
> difficult for children with learning problems -
> most often not out of malice, although their
> comments may seem malicious, but because they
> are not informed and do not understand. Ignor-
> ance is regrettable, but it is not incurable.

The parents' obligation to understand, and then to support is present from the start of any problem. The professional's obligation to inform the parent - carefully, thoroughly, with every tool at hand - is there from the start too.

QUESTIONS FOR INDIVIDUAL STUDY AND CLASS DISCUSSION

1. In counseling with parents of a child with a learning disability, it seems evident that one or both parents are
   placing too much pressure on the child to learn. How might
   you explore this topic and help them to an awareness of
   the danger or harm that may come about as a result of their
   "pressurized" approach? What factors do you consider
   important either to mention or lead into?

2. Invite a learning disabilities teacher to your class or
   group to discuss the procedures in counseling parents.

3. What counseling skills are necessary in order to insure
   that each parent is as thoroughly briefed, educated, and
   informed as each professional can make him.

4. Formulate your own definition of a learning disability that would be non-technical and relatively easy for parents to understand.

5. The parents of a child with a learning disability ask you to suggest outside reading material to help them understand their child's problem. What will you recommend that they read? What is the rationale for your selection(s).

6. Survey your local school system regulations and procedures pertaining to services for children with learning disabilities. Factors to include in your survey should include facilities, eligibility and placement, and types of programs. What definition do they use to determine what constitutes a learning disability?

7. Select any learning disability (perception problem, sensory-motor dysfunction, visual perception problem, perseveration, etc.) and after carefully describing the nature and degree of the learning disorder, devise a home-management program for parents to assist in the remediation of the disability. What questions would you anticipate from the parents? Is your home management program practical? Realistic? Founded on learning theory or mere speculation about what is best? Will outside professional help be needed? If so, will it be available?

8. Do you agree or disagree with the comments of Barsch and McCarthy and McCarthy that working with the child with a learning disability may differ from other handicapping conditions?

9. Parents ask you to explain how they will know if their child has a learning disability. In layman's language, how will you explain the diagnostic procedure? What types of testing or test battery might they expect?

10. What tests or assessment measurements would you select in diagnosing a child with learning disabilities? In selecting these, consider those tests which enjoy the greatest degree of validity, reliability, and predictability.

11. The emotions of parents of handicapped children are individual and complex and best known only by those who have experienced them. What value does this statement have for the counselor working with parents of children with learning disabilities? What do you see as the implications of the above statement?

12. Trace the history of parent involvement in bringing about constructive changes and services for children with learning disabilities.

13. Parents with whom you are counseling refuse to accept the fact (based on a complete and accurate diagnosis) that their child has a learning disability. As a concerned professional, what recourse do you have?

14. Because learning disabilities differ so much in kind and degree from individual to individual, would you advocate group counseling for parents of children with learning disabilities?

REFERENCES

1. Gearheart, B.R. Education of the Exceptional Child: History, Present Practices, and Trends. Scranton, Pen.: Intext Educational Publishers, 1972, p. 185.

2. Kirk, S.A. Educating Exceptional Children. 2nd Edition. Boston: Houghton Mifflin, 197, p. 43.

3. National Advisory Committee on Handicapped Children, First Annual Report, Subcommittee on Education of the Committee on Labor and Public Welfare, U.S. Senate. Washington, D.C.: U.S. Government Printing Office, 1968, p. 14.

4. McCarthy, J. & McCarthy, J. Learning Disabilities. Boston: Allyn & Bacon, 1969, p. 8.

5. Telford, C.W. & Sawrey, J.M. The Exceptional Individual. Englewood Cliffs: New Jersey: Prentice-Hall, 1972, p. 282.

6. Lerner, J.W. Children with Learning Disabilities: Theories, Diagnosis and Teaching Strategies. Boston: Houghton Mifflin, 1971, pp. 45-46.

7. Lerner, p. 47.

8. Barsch, R.H. The Parent Teacher Partnership. Arlington, Virginia: The Council for Exceptional Children, 1969, p. 5.

9. McCarthy & McCarthy, pp. 107-108.

10. Ellingson, C. The Shadow Children. Chicago: Topaz Books, 1967, p. 6.

11. Brown, G.W. "Suggestions for Parents," Journal of Learning Disabilities, 2, No. 2, (February, 1969), 97-106.

12. Bryant, J.E. "Parent-Child Relationships: Their Effect on Rehabilitation," Journal of Learning Disabilities, 6, No. 2, (February 1973), 102-105.

13. Neifert, J.T. & Gayton, W.F. "Parents and The Home Program Approach in the Remediation of Learning Disabilities," Journal of Learning Disabilities, 2, No. 2, (February, 1973), 85-89.

14. DeGenaro, J.J. "What Do You Say When a Parent Asks, How Can I Help My Child?" Journal of Learning Disabilities, 6, No. 2, February, 1973), 102-105.

15. Munsey, M. "The Parents' Right to Read," Journal of Learning Disabilities. 6, No. 6, (June/July, 1973), 394.

Chapter 10

COUNSELING PARENTS OF CHILDREN WITH
BEHAVIORAL DISORDERS

One might ask - is counseling parents of children with behavioral disorders really any different than working with parents of any other type of handicapped child? The answer is yes because of at least one basic distinction. The child who is blind, mentally retarded, or physically handicapped ordinarily results from factors which are not related to the relationship between the child and his parents or his environment. Ross [1] points out the difference in counseling focus by saying that "with parents of a physically handicapped or mentally retarded child the focus of counseling was on helping the parents cope with the fact that their child had a condition which, though often amenable to modification through educational, medical, or habilitative efforts, was largely a permanent state, potentially affecting the entire life cycle of the family." Ross adds that emotional disturbances, particularly in young children, can be treated and often cured so that work with the parents is aimed, not at helping them live with a chronic problem, but in aiding them to contribute to the child's treatment by making modifications in their own response patterns. There is a general consensus of opinion that a child's emotional disturbance is frequently, but not always, associated with the complex and intricate interpersonal relations within the family and the interactions that the family has within the larger social system.

Origins of Behavior Problems

As in other areas of exceptionality, the counselor should be knowledgeable about both the origins and characteristics of behavioral disorders. In examining the causes of behavior problems, it should be kept in mind that any etiology or cause is only assumed to be true and that there is always the possibility that any diagnosis will have to be changed. To compound the problem, many different diagnostic categories and ways of viewing the problem exist. In fact, the study of emotional disorders has proven to be exceedingly baffling and complex because of the very nature of man. Accurate diagnosis requires professional skills and knowledge because of the complex medical, environmental, and psychological causes, and further because the symptoms are often similar to those found in mental retardation and delinquency.

Many professional organizations are currently working toward more generally accepted systems of definition and diagnostic categories. The Report of the Joint Commission on Mental Health of Children [2] points out that when emotional and mental disorders are viewed in terms of their origins, five major categories can be distinguished: (1) faulty training, and faulty life experiences; (2) surface conflicts between children and parents which arise from such adjustment tasks as relations among siblings, school, social, and sexual development; (3) deeper conflicts which become internalized within the self and create emotional conflicts within the child (these are the so-called neuroses); (4) difficulties associated with physical handicaps and disorders; (5) difficulties associated with severe mental disorders, such as the psychoses. It is estimated that 80 percent of emotional problems are related to the first two categories, 10 percent to the third category, and 10 percent to the fourth and fifth.

Characteristics of the Emotionally Disturbed Child

Failure to recognize symptoms of disturbances as well as incorrect diagnosis can complicate the problem since the appropriateness of the method of treatment has a vital bearing on its success. Classroom teachers as well as parents may be able to identify these disturbed children. Generally speaking, any child having difficulty in adjusting to some aspect of his environment to such a degree that special help is needed is said to have a behavioral disorder. The behaviorally disordered child may exhibit any or some of the following difficulties:

1. Emotional disturbance which prohibits adjustment to everyday surroundings.

2. Inability to achieve satisfactory social relationships with peers and/or adults.

3. Disregard for accepted social values and rules.

4. Aggressive behavior, truancy, fighting, and defiance of authority.

5. Immature and/or withdrawn behavior.

6. An unexplained inability to learn. The child's difficulty cannot be explained adequately by intellectual deficits, specific learning disabilities, or by difficulties in cultural or ethnic background.

7. Hyperactivity, destructive and anti-social behavior.

8. A general pervasive mood of unhappiness or depression.

Most children have some of these behavior symptoms at various times. It must be emphasized that only those children who exhibit these difficulties over a sustained period of time would be so classified as behaviorally disordered children. Emotional disturbance is suspected when the symptoms persist and are marked enough to warrant special care, treatment, and education. For example, an occasional fight might be typical for most children, but when fights occur daily the behavior is maladaptive.

In addition, however, children who are experiencing crisis situations such as a death in the family, the divorce of parents, severe illness, school expulsions, school suspension, or problems involving social and/or correctional agencies may also need supportive assistance.

Blackham and Silberman [3] contend that the decision to change a child's behavior should involve at least three criteria. First, the behavior presumed to be maladaptive must occur with sufficient frequency. Second, the behavior, if continued, will ultimately end up being hurtful to the child and/or the environment. Third, the behavior impedes subsequent adaption and healthy development; for instance, excessively dependent or infantile behavior poses serious problems at later ages and developmental periods.

The Role of the Counselor in Professional Treatment

Because emotional disturbances are of varying degrees, they may be appropriately handled or treated in a variety of ways by a variety of personnel. It is, therefore, imperative that the counselor secure or be able to make a sufficient diagnosis. This being completed, the counselor should be a decision-maker in terms of what action to recommend to the pa-

rents. As a general rule, when the disturbances are transitory
and mild enough to be amenable to counseling, they may be handled by a number of professional persons who work with children: pediatricians and general practitioners, probation of-
ficers, child welfare and other social workers, teachers and
school counselors, public health and school nurses, and mini-
sters.

More serious disturbances are normally handled by members
of the mental health professions including psychiatrists, psychologists, and psychiatric social workers. A Child Guidance
Clinic may offer evaluation and treatment services to children
whose emotional disturbances are serious enough to warrant professional attention but not so advanced as to require full-
time psychiatric care. The counselor must use professional
judgment in determining the degree of difficulty and the proper referral.

Parental Reactions, Attitudes, and Concerns

Love [4] says that even with the greatest desire to aid
the emotionally disturbed child, the parents may run into very
difficult problems. One thing that is extremely important to
think about is the other children in the family. What about
their own anger and hostility and feelings of deprivation when
they are unable to bring their friends home or live normally
in their own home? What about the parent's feeling of guilt?
All these factors have to be considered by all the people concerned. Love adds that just as there is no "typical" family,
there is no family with an emotionally disturbed child like
any other.

Parents of emotionally handicapped children must learn to
deal with situations and conditions which parents of other
children never encounter, and this learning is not easy. They
often require as much help as the child. As in other handicapping conditions, the parents are just as concerned as the
physicians or the teacher, but are often unable to adequately
express their fears or worries. In working with parents of
children with behavioral disorders, parents need professional
support to help them feel competent and to assist them in
learning to make correct decisions. Only as parents are helped
to work through their problems can they achieve real peace of
mind.

113

When a child does not conform to the image of the "normal" child, then the parents must adapt their expectations and behaviors to the exceptional state of their child. The difficulty stems from the fact that at the same time they are learning to adapt to their expectations, they must also be able to help the child cope with his present condition. The counselor has a responsibility of assisting both the parent and child in making this difficult adjustment.

The Parent and Home Management Techniques

The parent of a child with a behavioral disorder can usually profit from assistance and direction in home management techniques. As one parent [5] has described his situation, "In helping our disturbed child to acceptable behavior, we found the most necessary characteristics that we as parents had to possess and show Jimmy were persistence, firmness, and joy (joy in his improvement, joy in our growth with him). Patience did not come simple without understanding of the problem. We had to learn patience through the menial, never-ending repetitious tasks that had to be done."

Maintaining a consistent pattern of firmness or discipline is often an essential part of the total responsibility these parents have in caring for their child with emotional conflicts. There is, of course, no "one way" to maintain discipline, but the counselor and professional have the responsibility to help the child unlearn his anger. Through discipline, tempered with love, parents must teach their children to behave in an acceptable manner.

Parents must not only hold the child to the correct course of action, they must also illustrate by example. This may be extremely difficult for many parents, but when discipline is reasonable and understandable, and even when the parents' behavior is inconsistent, he will love and respect them, even though his surface behavior may not always show it.

With proper guidance and direction, parents can become effective behavior modifers, especially in dealing with overt behaviors. Madsen and Madsen [6] suggest four principles for the parent:

1. Pinpoint: It is necessary to pinpoint explicitly the behavior that is to be eliminated or established. Do not deal with intangibles or ideas. If the behavior

cannot in some way be both observed and measured, then you can never know if it has been either established or unlearned.

2. Record: List the specified behaviors in time intervals and thereby provide a precise record from which to proceed. Keep the record accurate. Do not guess; be specific.

3. Consequate: Set up the external environmental contingencies (including primarily your own personal response) and proceed with the program. Contingencies include approval, withdrawal of approval, disapproval, threat of disapproval, or ignoring. Reinforcement techniques may be words (spoken-written), expressions (facial-bodily), closeness (nearness-touching), activities (social-individual), and things (food-play-things-money).

4. Evaluate: Be prepared to stay with a program long enough to ascertain its effectiveness. Compare records after consequeting with records taken before. Is the behavior increasing, decreasing, or remaining the same? Learn from your mistakes.

In assisting parents to pinpoint and identify various behaviors, the following check list of items may be presented to the parents during a parent interview. This information may also be useful in a general discussion of the child's behavior patterns and the attitudes of the parents toward their child.

1. Health and Physical Information. Describe any Problems:

Vision _____   Hearing _____

Speech _____   Motor Coordination _____

_____ Short Attention Span	_____ Acts Sad or Depressed
_____ Overactive	_____ Difficulty Concentrating
_____ Daydreams	_____ Selfish
_____ Quarrelsome	_____ Temper Outbursts
_____ Excitable	_____ Overly Sensitive
_____ Acts "Smart"	_____ Tattles
_____ Lacks Sense	_____ Extremely Shy
of Humor	_____ Highly Aggressive
	_____ Disturbs Other Children

2. Social Interaction

_____ Plays With Younger Neighborhood Children
_____ Plays With Children His Own Age
_____ Likes To Join In Group Activities
_____ Does Not Like To Join In Group Activities
_____ Children Don't Like To Play With Him (her)
_____ Fights A Lot With Other Children
_____ Teases Other Kids
_____ Likes To Break Up Other Children's Fun
_____ Usually Is The Leader In A Group
_____ Is Easily Led By A Group

3. Attitude Toward Parents:

_____ Demands Attention   _____ Acts Like A Spoiled
      Much Of The Time   Brat Much Of The
_____ Submissive (Does   Time
      Whatever He's Told   _____ Always Wants To Do
      Whenever He's Told   Something To Please
      To Do It)   You
_____ Doesn't Do Anything   _____ Doesn't Seem To
      He's Told To Do   Care About Much
_____ Cries When Scolded   Of Anything
      Or Told He's Done   _____ Doesn't Seem To
      Something Wrong   Like School
_____ Scared Of A Lot   _____ Is Very Stubborn
      Of Things   _____ Is Very Shy

4. Does Your Child Exhibit Any Of The Following Behaviors?

_____ Nail Biting   _____ Stuttering   _____ Excessive
_____ Lisping   _____ Stealing   Eye Blinking
_____ Trembling   _____ Sex Problems   _____ Crying
_____ Stomach Aches   _____ Unusual   _____ Bedwetting
                             Behavior

Explain Any Of The Above That Have Been Checked. _____

_____

_____

116

5. What do you do when your child does something he's been told not to do?

   Father: _____

   _____

   Mother: _____

   _____

6. What Goals Do You Have For Your Child?

   Father: _____

   _____

   Mother: _____

   _____

7. How Would You Feel About Special Class Placement For Your Child?

   Father: _____

   _____

   Mother: _____

   _____

It is also important for the counselor or professional to help parents realize it is their responsibility – not the child's – to insure that proper learning actually takes place. Through trial and error and through a professional who will lend encouragement and assistance in the understanding of behavioral principles, parents of the emotionally disturbed child can find better ways to stimulate their children toward optimum adjustment and patterns of behavior.

Recognizing Feelings

Much of the literature stresses the importance of being objective with a parent of a "problem" child, but this does not mean that feelings must be absent. It does mean that feelings must be recognized and kept from distorting interpersonal perceptions. It should also be remembered that many parents tend to reject unpleasant or painful information which comes from a seemingly uninterested or unfeeling source. Given a supportive, warm, professional relationship, most parents are frank in admitting that there is a problem and are not so concerned with the "who" and "why" (since most never find out anyway), but are more concerned with "What are we going to do about it?" As a prospective counselor or professional working with the parent of a child with behavioral disorders, what will you be prepared to do that will bring about constructive behavior changes?

QUESTIONS FOR INDIVIDUAL STUDY AND CLASS DISCUSSION

1. Do you think that poverty conditions may cause higher rates of emotional disturbance?

2. As a research topic, identify various schools of thought that seek to explain the causes of behavioral disorders - such as those that stress constitutional factors present in the child at birth.

3. In the past decade, a shift in thinking has occurred within the mental health professions and there is today less focus on psychological conflicts and more concentration on the social, familial, and cultural factors. Do you agree with this trend? What implications does this have for the counselor of parents of emotionally disturbed children?

4. Can you develop or think of ways to devise a more adequate system of classification of emotionally disturbed children that would include, but not necessarily be limited to, an evaluation of assets and deficiencies of the child and of the ecological system of which he is a part?

5. List some advantages for a comprehensive psychoeducational assessment that is interdisciplinary in nature for the child with behavioral disorders.

6. Should diagnostic data be used exclusively to determine the treatment program of the child or should they serve only as guidelines? What value would you place on professional opinions and ideas based on other information (such as what service the parents prefer that the child be offered and what is available)?

7. Why is it essential that diagnosis should be an on-going process?

8. Do you maintain that the personalities of the parents cause the child's difficulties or that the child's inherent personality traits cause the parents to react to him in unacceptable ways?

9. What methods can be used to counsel the parents who admit there's a problem, and then proceed to blame someone else, or themselves?

10. Do you think that the "professional" too often forgets that parents are people? Can this be corrected? If so, how?

11. Do you think that our graduate schools of psychology, social work, and education are teaching future diagnosticians, therapists, and teachers the basic essentials that are really known about deviant learning and behavior problems?

12. Do you think that professionals frequently underestimate the expertise of the parent - expertise in the sense of who really knows best in terms of his own experiences about what it means to be the parent of a child with a behavioral disorder?

13. What valid reasons may be given to explain why emotional disorders, particularly in children, are often difficult for parents to understand, recognize, and accept.

14. Make a list of agencies and school (public and private) in your community, city, county, or state, that offer services adequate both in quality and quantity to assure that children and youth with behavioral disorders can secure proper diagnosis and treatment.

15. In terms of definition and characteristics, how does the child who is socially maladjusted differ from the child who is emotionally disturbed?

16. Explore the current needs in your state for trained teachers of the emotionally disturbed. What colleges and/or universities offer undergraduate and graduate programs? What does a typical program consist of in terms of requirements and courses?

REFERENCES

1. Ross, A.O. The Exceptional Child in the Family. New York: Grune & Stratton, 1964, pp. 145-146.

2. Crisis in Child Mental Health: Challenge for the 1970's. Report of the Joint Commission on Mental Health of Children. New York: Harper & Row, 1969, p. 251.

3. Blackham, G.J. & Silberman, A. Modification of Child Behavior. Belmont, California: Wadsworth Publishing Co., 1971, p. 3.

4. Love, H.D. Parental Attitudes Toward Exceptional Children. Springfield, Ill.: Charles C. Thomas, 1970, p. 119.

5. Tomaro, M.S. "Learning to Live Happily With Jimmy," The Exceptional Parent, I, No. 6 (April/May 1972), 37.

6. Madsen, C.K., & Madsen, C.H. Parents/Children/Discipline: A Positive Approach. Boston: Allyn & Bacon, 1972, p. 32.

Chapter 11

COUNSELING PARENTS OF THE GIFTED CHILD

The counselor of parents of exceptional children must not only be concerned with the handicapped child, but should also be aware of the nature and characteristics of the gifted child. There is no one acknowledged authority for the definition of such children although certain generalizations are accepted by the majority of educators and researchers. These generalizations include factors of early physical and mental development and rapid learning ability. Drews [1] published a list of characteristics that many other writers have included in their identification criteria:

1. Early physical and mental development.

2. Curiosity, alertness, interest in many things, a desire to be informed.

3. Interest in books, especially reference books - dictionaries, encyclopedias, atlases, biographies.

4. Pursuit of an interest over a long period of time and with intense concentration.

5. Easy and rapid learning.

6. Enjoyment of abstractions - generalizations, making analyses, handling complexities, and using flexible divergent approaches.

7. Qualities of leadership and responsibility.

8. Reading, computation, and communicating with ease.

The Report to the Congress by the U.S. Commissioner of Education [2] not only adds credibility to the quest for an acceptable definition, but also illustrates the expanding concept of giftedness. Public Law 91-230, Section 806, states that the Commissioner of Education shall define "gifted and talented" for the purposes of Federal education programs. The definition established by the advisory panel reads:

Gifted and talented children are those identified by professionally qualified persons who
by virtue of outstanding abilities, are capable
of high performance. These are children who
require differentiated education programs and/
or services beyond those normally provided by
the regular school program in order to realize their contribution to self and society.

Children capable of high performance include those with demonstrated achievement and/or potential ability in any of the
following areas, singly or in combination:

1. general intellectual ability
2. specific academic aptitude
3. creative or productive thinking
4. leadership ability
5. visual and performing arts
6. psychomotor ability

In an effort to establish specific criteria for the identification of the creative child, Torrance [3] defines creative thinking as fluency (large number of ideas), flexibility (variety of different approaches or categories of ideas),
sensitivity to defects and problems, and redefinition (per-
ceiving in a way different from the usual, established or intended way or use.)

If a definition had to be given in one sentence, Hildreth's
[4] would probably be as suitable as any other: "We might gen-
eralize by saying that the gifted child or young person is one
whose development and behavior - apart from sheer physical superiority - consistently demonstrates unusual traits, capaci-
ties and achievements for his age."

It is interesting to note that the 1970 report of the U.S.
Commissioner of Education states that a conservative estimate
of the gifted and talented population ranges between 1.5 and
2.5 million children out of total elementary and secondary
school population of 51.6 million. It can be readily seen
that the gifted constitute a sizeable portion of our exceptional child population.

General Counseling Goals

The counselor's understanding of the characteristics of

the gifted child is important, but the greater task lies in working toward improvement of the parents' understanding of gifted children and youth in general and their own children in particular. As Gowan and Demos [5] have stated: "It is necessary not only for them to understand him [the gifted child] and encourage his school progress, it is also important that parents understand that they have a special stake in his future, and, as such, should be expected to provide some of the special advantages from which he will profit and not leave it all to the school."

Laycock [6] suggests that those who counsel the parents of the gifted need to proceed on certain basic assumptions:

1. The gifted child is, first of all, a child. Parents ofteh need help in seeing their exceptional youngster as, first of all, a child with a child's problems of development as he advances through the various stages from infancy to maturity. Parents need help in seeing their child's growth in its totality -emotional, social, and physical as well as intellectual. They need to know that their gifted youngster. in his growing up, is faced with development tasks of all children -in early, middle and late childhood and adolescence-and that he may be exceptional only in his intellectual growth or special talents.

2. The gifted child is a unique individual rooted in a certain family, community and culture. Gifted children cannot be sterotyped. While certain general principles apply to their guidance, each child differs from his gifted fellows. He is unique in his innate characteristics and in the way he interacts with his own family circle, with his community, and with the culture of his own nation and of the contemporary world.

3. The gifted child, like all children, has four sets of teachers - home teachers, playmate teachers, school teachers, and community teachers (church, Sunday school, Scouts, movies, radio, television, recreational facilities, and the standards held by the adults of the commuunity).

For the child's best development there must be close cooperation between his different sets of teachers - certainly between his home, school, and community teachers.

Parents of gifted children are human beings with emotional problems of their own and need a good measure of self-understanding. Parents of bright youngsters may, like any parent, suffer from feelings of insecurity and inadequacy or they may posses deep-seated feelings of hostility and resentment. They need help not only in understanding why their children act as they do, but also in understanding why they themselves react to their children the way they do. Otherwise they may exploit their gifted child, resent him, be jealous of him, or overdominate or over-protect him.

While the gifted child is more likely to have a superior adjustment than the average child, psychological, personality, or educational problems may arise and necessitate the need for timely preventive or remedial actions. In this event, the parent seeking help usually has three options at his disposal. He may help his gifted child through individual efforts or turn to a counselor or other trained person such as a school psychologist, or he may find assistance through involvement and the obtaining of information from associations such as the National Association for the Gifted Children (NACC) and The Association for the Gifted (TAG) of the Council for Exceptional Children.

Fostering Creativity

One of the central responsibilities of the counselor who seeks to help parents of a creative child is to assist them in cultivating and developing creativity. What guide lines can we recommend? Gowan and Torrance [7] offer some practical suggestions:

1. Do not set up unconscious unfavorable evaluation, upgrade rather than belittle the child's concept of his ability to create while remaining relatively realistic about valuing products.

2. Provide a warm and safe psychological base from

which to explore and to which the child may return when he is frightened by his own discoveries.

3. Be tolerant yourself of new ideas. Be respectful of children's curiosity and questioning, and ideas.

4. Help children name and classify things. In helping children value their ideas attach meaning, worth and value to as many ideas and life experiences as possible.

5. Creative children are self-starters, with high-energy, humor, independences and initiative. These can be hindered by too much supervision. Let the child be alone as he wishes, and carry things out on his own.

6. Heighten sensory awareness of children by helping them to value and enjoy sensory percepts and experiences without guilt. Point out to him beauty of the simple, the job of observing nature closely, the delight in crafts and mastery of a discipline, etc.

7. Think what people do to stamp out creativity - then do the opposite. Think of various authoritian attitudes; conventionalism, aggression, submission, anti-intraception, stereotyping, projectivity, then try to behave oppositely.

8. Respect individual differences. Don't just merely tolerate.

Motivating and Developing Talent in the Gifted Child

Havinghurst [8] suggests that only about half of the ablest 20 percent of gifted children actually develop their abilities to a point where they make an important contribution to society. The critical question is - Who are the other half, and why do they not develop their talents more fully? The general answer to this question is that those with underdeveloped talent are persons whose environments have been least favorable to the product of high level ability.

125

Children from low-status families often fail to develop their abilities because of lack of opportunity and stimulation. Of course, this may also hold true for families from upper socio-economic levels. The quality of life experiences at home, the nature of parent guidance and controls, as well as life in the neighborhood all influence the gifted child's intellectual, social, and emotional development. This is to suggest that the parents set the example for the young child's growth and responsibilities to a greater extent than any other influence. The reader should immediately grasp the significance of this state of affairs. The counselor must be able to offer parents concrete suggestions so as to encourage an optimum home environment. Many of the traditional failings of the gifted child are due largely to poor guidance and management and this can be counteracted by taking certain precautions in home training. In many instances, parents are overprotective or overanxious, and the counselor must help them overcome their undue concern so that the child can gain more confidence. The child who comes from a home with understanding and supportive parents who work as partners with teachers is more likely to attain his ultimate goal and, in the final analysis, make a contribution to self and society.

What are some constructive ways in which the counselor can assist parents of exceptional children? Gowan* [9] gives many practical suggestions for parents of the gifted children:

1. They are still children. They need love but controls; attention but discipline; parental involvement, yet training in self-dependence and responsibility.

2. Consonance of parental value systems is important for their optimum development. This means that there should not be wide disagreements over values between parents.

3. Parental involvement in early task demands, such as training them to perform tasks themselves, to count, tell time, use correct vocabulary and pronunciation, locate themselves and get around their neighborhood, do errands and be responsible are all important.

---

*Reprinted by permission of the author and The Gifted Child Quarterly.

4. Emphasis on early verbal expression, reading, discussing ideas in the presence of children, poetry and music are all valuable. Parents should read to children. There should be an emphasis by parents on doing well in school.

5. The lack of disruption of family life through divorce or separation, and the maintenance of a happy, healthy home is an important aspect in raising able children, as well as other children.

6. Since able children often have vague awareness of adult problems such as sex, death, sickness, finances, war, etc. which their lack of experiences makes them unable to solve, they may need reassurance in these areas.

7. Parents can see to it that the gifted child age six or above has a playmate who is able, even if he has to be "imported" from some distance.

8. The role of good books, magazines and other aids to home learning, such as encyclopedias, charts, collections, etc. is important.

9. Parents should take the initiative in taking able children to museums, art galleries, educational institutions and other historical places where collections of various sorts may enhance background learning.

10. Parents should be especially careful not to "shut up" the gifted child who asks questions. In particular, he should not be scolded for asking, nor should it be inferred that this is an improper or forbidden subject. The parent may, however, insist that questions not be asked at inappropriate times, and he may require the child to sharpen or rephrase his questions so as to clarify it. Sometimes questions should not be answered completely, but the reply should itself be a question which sends the child into some larger directions. When the parent cannot answer the questions, he should direct the child to a resource which can.

Sometimes questions call for clarification of concepts, as with the young child who asked, "Why aren't all these rockets liable to shoot down God?"

11. There's a difference between pushing and intellectual stimulation. Parents should avoid "pushing" a child into reading, "exhibiting" him before others or courting undue publicity about him. On the other hand, parents should seek in every way to stimulate and widen the child's mind, through suitable experiences in books, recreation, travel and the arts.

12. The gifted child usually has a wide and versatile range of interests, but he may be somewhat less able to concentrate on one area for a long time. Parents should encourage children who have hobbies to follow through on them, to plan and strive for creditable performance and for real mastery, rather than "going through" a lot of hobbies or collections in a short time.

13. Parents should avoid direct, indirect or unspoken attitudes that fantasy, orginality, unusual questions, imaginary playmates, or out-of-ordinary mental processes on the part of the child are bad, "different" or to be discouraged. Instead of laughing at the child, laugh with him and seek to develop his sense of humor.

14. Parents can avoid overstructuring children's lives so that they don't have any free time. Sometimes parents are concerned that gifted children spend some time in watching TV or reading comic books. While they should not spend all their time in doing so, they cannot be expected to perform at top capacity at all times.

15. Respect the child, and his knowledge, which at times may be better than your own and impatient of authority. Assume that he means to do right, and that deviations are not intentional.

Do not presume on your authority as a parent except in crises. Allow much liberty on unimportant issues. Try to give him general instructions to carry out in his way rather than specific commands to carry out in yours.

16. Gifted children are sometimes impatient of conventions. Have a frank talk with your child about the importance of conventions, such as driving on the right hand side, where he can see the social advantages, and then point out that other conventions of politeness, manners, courtesy and regard for others have similar bases in experience.

17. Whenever possible talk things out with him where there has been a disciplinary lapse. He is much more amenable to rational argument than are many children and usually has a well-developed sense of duty.

18. Give him the stimulation of private lessons in some skill in which he excels. See that he has social membership in worthy groups. Foster special experiences outside the home by his traveling alone, or visiting friends overnight. Try to facilitate his chance to talk alone with an adult authority in some line that interests him.

19. Try to improve his sense of taste in mass media, TV, radio, cinema, newspapers, comics, reading, art, etc. Discuss the basis for taste and give him some experience with new forms of expression in the arts.

20. Take time to be with him, to listen to what he has to say, to discuss ideas with him.

21. Be a good example yourself, and try to find worthy adult model figures of both sexes outside his family for him to know.

22. Support the school efforts to plan for able children. Help to interest the PTA in the problem.

Support study groups on gifted children. Form with other parents into cooperative endeavors.

23. Investigate scholarship programs of your community for other gifted children and help provide them.

24. Work to provide better community understanding of, and appreciation of, the role of the able child in society and the importance of community planning.

25. Support community action for able children, including bonds and school taxes for extra educational advantages. Advocate more guidance and special education for the gifted.

In concluding this chapter, A Creed for a Parent of a Gifted Child [10] is presented in hopes that both counselors and parents will more fully understand and appreciate the gifted child.

I, _____, do honestly and lovingly swear, as a parent of the gifted, to know, understand, tolerate, accept, and give attention, support and regard to those manifestations of his individuality: I promise to create an environment, in the home and without, which will best guide, direct, and help my child fulfill the highest positive levels of his intellectual, emotional and physical growth: I pledge to seek for my child those educational experiences, including excellence in teachers, schools, and communities, which will offer the greatest opportunities to my child from which, hopefully, will emerge a worthwhile and a meaningful contribution to society and to himself.

QUESTIONS FOR INDIVIDUAL STUDY AND CLASS DISCUSSION

1. Survey your community, city or state for services provided for gifted children. What is the nature and scope of these services?

2. Interview parents of gifted children. What types of problems, concerns and special challenges did or does their gifted child present to them? Was counseling available if and when they needed it?

3. Write or contact the Association for the Gifted (TAG) of the Council for Exceptional Children (CEC), and the National Association for Gifted Children (NAGC) for information as to their purposes, goals, membership, and meetings. What are the similarities and differences in these organizations? How might parents of a gifted child profit from membership in these organizations?

4. How would one go about initiating and organizing a parent group dedicated to the understanding and advancement of gifted children?

5. Discuss any ways you can think of which differentiate basic differences as to how the counselor would work with parents of the gifted child. Do you take the position that the counseling skills and processes are essentially the same? If not, how do they differ?

6. As a generalization, would you agree or disagree that parents of gifted children are confronted with as many problems and concerns as parents of handicapped children? What factors account for your response? Does the research and literature offer any evidence to support or refute your contention?

7. Why is it important for parents not to exaggerate their child's superiority or make him unduly conscious of it? What course of action can they take in this respect?

8. How might the counselor assist parents to listen to their child with insight and understanding?

9. One school of thought contends that the gifted are our most "handicapped" population. Do you agree or disagree? What reasons can you offer to support your view?

10. Do you have a broad or narrow view of what constitutes giftedness? How might this affect a counseling relationship with parents?

11. Devise a family enrichment program for parents of an intellectually gifted child.

REFERENCES

1. Drews, E.M., Bish, C.E., Cotlove, E., and Hitchcock, A.A.,
    Guidance for the Academically Talented Student. Na-
    tional Education Association Project on the Academi-
    cally Talented Student and American Personnel and
    Guidance Association. Washington, D.C., 1961, p. 96.

2. Education of the Gifted and Talented, Report to the Congress
    of the United States by the U.S. Commissioner of Edu-
    cation. March, 1972, p. 2.

3. Torrance, E.P., Gifted Children in the Classroom., The
    MacMillan Company, New York, 1965, p. 6.

4. Hildreth, G.H. Introduction to the Gifted. New York:
    McGraw-Hill, p. 572.

5. Gowan, J.C. and Demos, G.D., The Education and Guidance of
    the Ablest., Springfield, Ill., Charles C. Thomas, 1964.

6. Laycock, S.R. "Counseling Parents of Gifted Children,"
    Exceptional Children. (December, 1956), pp. 108-109.

7. Gowan, J.C., & Torrance, E.P., Educating the Ablest: A Book
    of Readings on the Education of Gifted Children.
    Itasca, Ill.: Peacock Publishers, 1971, pp. 180-181.

8. Havinghurst, R.H. "Conditions Favorable and Detrimental
    to the Development of Talent," School Review 65, No. 1
    (March, 1957), pp. 20-26.

9. Gowan, J.C. "Twenty-Five Suggestions for Parents of Able
    Children," The Gifted Child Quarterly. 8 (1964),
    pp. 192-93.

10. Harris, Darryl. "A Creed for a Parent of a Gifted Child,"
    Florida Association for the Gifted. Vol. 1, No. 1,
    December, 1973.

INDEX OF NAMES

INDEX OF SUBJECTS